The
Food Allergy News
Cookbook

❖❖

A Collection of Recipes
from *Food Allergy News* and
Members of The Food Allergy Network

Edited by Anne Muñoz-Furlong

John Wiley & Sons, Inc.
New York • Chichester • Weinheim • Brisbane • Singapore • Toronto

ISBN 0-471-34692-6

Printed in the United States of America

10 9 8 7 6 5 4

Contents

✦✦

The Food Allergy Network ✦ v

Getting Started ✦ 1

Breads and Breakfasts ✦ 13

Main Meals ✦ 57

Cookies and Snacks ✦ 85

Cakes, Pies, and Frostings ✦ 155

Miscellaneous Dishes ✦ 191

More Information ✦ 211

Glossary ✦ 213

Index ✦ 219

The following symbols are used throughout this cookbook to indicate recipes that are free from a food allergan.

◆ Milk-free

◆ Egg-free

◆ Wheat-free

◆ Peanut-free

◆ Soy-free

◆ Nut-free

The Food Allergy Network

✦✦

The Food Allergy Network is a nonprofit organization with members in the United States, Canada, and around the world. Food allergies affect 5% of children and 1–2% of adults. According to scientists, food allergy is the leading cause of fatal allergic reactions. Our mission is to increase public awareness about food allergy and anaphylaxis and to provide education, emotional support, and coping strategies to patients and their families.

A bimonthly newsletter is sent to all members as well as special mailings informing them of product information including ingredient changes, recalls, or packaging mishaps. Members include families, doctors, nurses, support group leaders, government agencies, and food manufacturers.

FAN was founded by Anne Muñoz-Furlong. Anne's daughter was diagnosed with milk and egg allergies as an infant. The lack of accurate information and practical support compelled Anne to establish a central clearinghouse of information for others.

For more information:

The Food Allergy Network
10400 Eaton Place, Suite 107
Fairfax, VA 22030-2208

1-800-929-4040
E-mail: fan@worldweb.net
Website: http://www.foodallergy.org

Getting Started

The recipes in this book use ingredients you probably already have at home or can find at the local grocery or health-food store. To increase the number of recipes available to you, try experimenting with these recipes by changing frostings, substituting flours, making cupcakes instead of cakes, adding fruit, and so on. Each time you change an ingredient, jot it down right on the recipe page and include comments and notes.

Allergy-free cooking can be challenging, stimulating, and fun. We hope many of these recipes will become family favorites.

If you are just getting started with allergy-free cooking, keep in mind that you will have to learn a whole new way of shopping and cooking. It will take time. You will have some successes, and you are going to make mistakes. Learn from each mistake, but never give up! Celebrate each success.

Shopping Tips

The only cure for food allergies is to avoid the food completely, therefore, you must read the labels on all foods. Furthermore, ingredients change without warning, so read labels each time you shop. This section includes lists of scientific and technical names for the foods that most commonly cause allergies. See the For More Information section to order these lists on wallet-size, laminated cards.

If the ingredients are not listed on a package, do not buy or eat the food. Avoid buying from bulk food bins; the chance for accidents from mislabeling or cross-contamination with other foods is not worth the money saved.

Kosher Symbols Can Help Make Shopping Easier

In a kosher kitchen, milk and meat products are never mixed. To ensure this is not done, the Jewish community has developed codes to indicate whether a product contains dairy products. The symbols are found on the front of the package near the product name. They will help anyone on a milk-free diet.

A "D" or "DE" (dairy equipment) listed next to the symbol for the kosher agency that checked the product (ⓚ, ⓤ, or others) means the product contains milk. A "D" or "DE" on a product that does not list milk in the ingredients may indicate that the food was contaminated by milk during processing.

These symbols are not found on all food products. However, by looking for products that have them, you will save time when searching for milk-free products.

Cooking Tips

Having the right equipment can make the difference between an enjoyable time in the kitchen or a time plagued by frustration. Take some time and organize your kitchen to ensure you enjoy your time there. Alphabetize your spices to save time searching through the cabinet to find that small jar of spice you thought you had.

Store the spices on a lazy Susan to make finding them easier. If you can find one with multiple tiers, you will be able to store many spices in a small area. The next time you shop, buy a variety of spices and extracts that you might not always have on hand, for example, apple pie spice or mace. It's wonderful to try new recipes without having to make a trip to the store for spices or extracts. Buy multiple sets of measuring spoons so you won't have to spend time washing your only set.

Experiment with your recipes. Try to cook the same foods for everyone in your family. If that is not possible, when cooking the allergy-free meals use separate utensils and pans to prevent traces of the "forbidden" food from contaminating the allergy-free meal.

Select one day a week to prepare a few meals and freeze them, or double the recipe when you cook and freeze half of it. While preparing another meal, cook foods that require a long time to bake or simmer, such as spaghetti sauce.

Tools You Can Use

Treat yourself. Since you're going to spend more time in the kitchen, buy yourself these time savers: an electric blender, mini or regular size food processor, microwave oven, waffle iron, non-stick griddle, muffin tins in various sizes, and a bread machine.

Let us know about gadgets you find useful. You are not alone; we're all in this together. I hope you enjoy this cookbook.

How to Read a Label for a Milk-Free Diet

This is a partial list of foods to avoid for a milk-free diet:

- artificial butter flavor
- butter, butter fat, butter oil, buttermilk
- casein
- caseinates (ammonium, calcium, magnesium, potassium, sodium)
- cheese
- cottage cheese
- cream
- curds
- custard
- half-and-half
- hydrolysates (casein, milk protein, protein, whey, whey protein)
- lactalbumin, lactalbumin phosphate
- lactoglobulin
- lactose

- milk (derivative, protein, solids, malted, condensed, evaporated, dry, whole, low-fat, nonfat, skimmed, and goat's milk)
- nougat
- pudding
- rennet casein
- sour cream, sour cream solids, sour milk solids
- whey (delactosed, demineralized, protein concentrate)
- yogurt

Label ingredients that may indicate the presence of milk protein:

- Flavorings including: caramel, bavarian cream, coconut cream, brown sugar, butter, natural
- chocolate
- high-protein flour
- luncheon meat, hot dogs, sausages
- margarine
- Simplesse
- A "D" on the front of a product label next to one of the symbols for Kosher agencies ((K), (U), and others) indicates the presence of milk protein. Some nondairy products contain casein and can cause a reaction.

How to Read a Label for an Egg-Free Diet

This is a partial list of the ingredient terms or foods to avoid for an egg-free diet:

- albumin
- egg (white, yolk, dried, powdered, solids)
- egg lecithin
- egg substitutes
- eggnog
- globulin
- livetin

- lysozyme (used in Europe)
- mayonnaise
- meringue
- ovalbumin
- ovomucin
- ovomucoid
- ovovitellin
- Simplesse

Be careful, a shiny glaze **or** yellow baked goods usually indicate the presence of eggs.

How to Read a Label for a Wheat-Free Diet

This is a partial list of the ingredient terms or foods to avoid for a wheat-free diet:

- bran
- bread crumbs
- bulgur
- cereal extract
- couscous
- cracker meal
- durum, durum flour
- enriched flour
- farina
- gluten
- graham flour
- high-gluten flour
- high-protein flour
- kamut
- seitan
- semolina

- soft wheat flour
- spelt
- vital gluten
- wheat (bran, germ, gluten, malt, starch)
- whole-wheat berries
- whole-wheat flour

Label ingredients that *may* indicate the presence of wheat protein:

- gelatinized starch
- hydrolyzed vegetable protein
- modified food starch
- modified starch
- natural flavoring
- soy sauce
- starch
- vegetable gum
- vegetable starch

How to Read a Label for a Peanut-Free Diet

This is a partial list of the ingredient terms or foods to avoid:

- beer nuts
- cold pressed peanut oil
- ground nuts
- mixed nuts
- Nu-Nuts flavored nuts
- peanut butter
- peanut flour
- peanuts

Foods that *may* contain peanut protein:

- African, Chinese, Vietnamese, Indonesian, and Thai dishes

- baked goods (pastries, cookies, etc.)
- candy
- chili
- chocolate (candies, candy bars)
- egg rolls
- hydrolyzed plant protein
- hydrolyzed vegetable protein
- marzipan
- nougat

Keep the following in mind:

- Peanuts are very allergenic and can cause an anaphylactic (general body) reaction.
- Studies show that most allergic individuals can safely eat peanut oil (not cold pressed peanut oil).

How to Read a Label for a Soy-Free Diet

This is a partial list of the ingredient terms or foods to avoid:

- hydrolyzed soy protein
- miso
- shoyu sauce
- soy (albumin, flour, grits, nuts, milk, sprouts)
- soybean (granules, curd)
- soy protein (concentrate, isolate)
- soy sauce
- Tamari
- tempeh
- textured vegetable protein (TVP)
- tofu

Label ingredients that *may* indicate the presence of soy protein:

- hydrolyzed plant protein

- hydrolyzed vegetable protein
- natural flavoring
- vegetable broth
- vegetable gum
- vegetable starch

Keep the following in mind:

- Studies show most soy-allergic individuals can safely eat soy lecithin and soy oil.

How to Read a Label for a Tree Nut Allergy

Below is a partial list of foods to avoid for a tree nut free diet:

- almonds
- Brazil nuts
- cashews
- chestnuts
- filbert/hazelnuts
- gianduja (a creamy mixture of chocolate and chopped toasted nuts found in premium or imported chocolate)
- hickory nuts
- macadamia nuts
- marzipan/almond paste
- nougat
- Nu-Nuts artificial nuts
- nut butters (e.g., cashew butter)
- nut meal
- nut oil
- nut paste (e.g., almond paste)
- pecans (including Mashuga® nuts)
- pine nuts (pinyons, Indian nuts)
- pistachios
- walnuts

Keep the following in mind:

- Nu-Nuts artificial nuts are peanuts that have been deflavored and reflavored with a nut, such as pecan or walnut.
- Filberts are also hazelnuts.

Substitutions

1 cup cake or pastry flour = 1 cup all-purpose flour less 2 tablespoons

1 teaspoon baking powder = 1/4 teaspoon baking soda plus 1/2 teaspoon cream of tartar

1 cup sugar = 1 cup honey (use 1/4 cup less liquid in recipe)

1 cup brown sugar = 1 cup granulated sugar

1 cup oil = 1/2 pound butter or margarine

Egg Substitutes

Use any one of the following combinations instead of eggs in baked foods. For each egg, use:

- 1 teaspoon baking powder, 1 tablespoon liquid, 1 tablespoon vinegar
- 1 teaspoon yeast dissolved in 1/4 cup warm water
- 1 tablespoon apricot purée
- 1 1/2 tablespoons water, 1 1/2 tablespoons oil, 1 teaspoon baking powder
- 1 packet plain gelatin, 2 tablespoons warm water. Do not mix until ready to use.
- For larger quantities that you can keep on hand, mix 1 envelope of unflavored gelatin with 1 cup boiling water. Substitute 3 tablespoons of this liquid gelatin for each egg in your recipe. (This mixture will not gel up as quickly as will the above mixture using a whole envelope with 2 tablespoons of water.) Refrigerate the remainder for up to a week, and microwave to liquefy for use in other recipes.

—Joyce Yokell

Milk Substitutes

In baking, for 1 cup milk, substitute 1 cup water or 1 cup allowed fruit juice such as apple or orange plus 1 tablespoon oil or shortening.

Note: Goat's milk protein is similar to cow's milk protein and may, therefore, cause a reaction in milk-allergic individuals.

Flour Substitutes

Wheat-, Gluten-, and Gliadin-Free Flour Gluten is found in the protein of certain grains, such as wheat, oats, barley, and rye. It can be broken down into two parts: gliadin and glutenin. Gliadin must be avoided by people with celiac sprue.

The flavor and texture of baked products can be different without gluten. Combining flours can make the product more acceptable. A gliadin-free (GF) flour mixture is an excellent substitute for wheat flour in your favorite recipe.

Use any of the following for a thickening agent instead of 1 tablespoon wheat flour:

- 1 1/2 teaspoons cornstarch
- 1 1/2 teaspoons potato starch flour
- 1 1/2 teaspoons arrowroot starch
- 1 tablespoon white or brown rice flour
- 2 teaspoons quick-cooking tapioca
- 1 1/2 teaspoons sweet rice flour

Gliadin-Free Flour Use any of the following when baking for a wheat- or gluten-free diet as a substitute for 1 cup wheat flour:

- 7/8 cup white or brown rice flour
- 5/8 cup potato starch flour
- 1 cup soy flour plus 1/4 cup potato starch flour
- 1/2 cup soy flour plus 1/2 cup potato starch flour
- 1 cup corn flour
- 1 scant cup fine cornmeal

Gluten-free flours do not rise as well as gluten flours. To make your baked foods rise better, mix baking powder or soda with water or other liquid in the recipe before adding it to other ingredients.

Xanthan Gum

Xanthan gum is added to salad dressings, canned gravies and sauces, and ice cream to give these foods a smoother texture. It also has the ability to hold food particles together well, which makes it a good stabilizer. It works well as a substitute for gluten in yeast breads. You can order xanthan gum from Ener-G Foods, listed in the For More Information section.

Hints for Using Xanthan Gum in Your Favorite Recipes Try the following proportions of xanthan gum to gluten-free flour for best results:

- Cakes: 1/4 teaspoon xanthan gum per 1 cup gluten-free flour

- Breads: 1 teaspoon xanthan gum per 1 cup gluten-free flour

- Pizza Crusts: 2 teaspoons xanthan gum per 1 cup gluten-free flour

—*Celiac Sprue Support Group*, Ohio Miami Valley Area

Flour: What's the Difference?

Arrowroot Arrowroot has a chalky taste but can be used successfully in foods such as puddings.

Barley Flour Barley flour has a mild flavor, but a heavier texture than wheat flour. It is good for quick breads, muffins, and cookies. It does not rise well in yeast products. Barley flour works well for cakes, and makes an excellent pie crust. It can be substituted cup for cup for regular flour.

Corn Flour Derived from corn, this flour blends well with cornmeal.

Cornstarch Cornstarch blends well with other flours, is a good thickening agent, and is good for use in pies and pie fillings.

Potato Flour Potato flour is a heavy flour with a potato taste. It has limited use as a single flour, but small amounts blended with other flours can be a good thickener.

Potato Starch Flour Potato starch flour is best combined with other flours in cookies and cakes. This flour works well as a thickening agent in place of cornstarch in soups, stews, gravies, and such. It is not good for breads or other baked goods.

Rice Flour Rice flour produces a grainy texture. Combine liquid in recipes with rice flour before mixing with other ingredients to produce a smoother product. Rice flour is excellent in gravies. To keep it fresh, refrigerate or freeze the flour. Sweet rice flour, available in Oriental food stores, can be substituted for part of the rice flour. You cannot bake with sweet rice flour, but it is an excellent thickener and is good for stir-fry dishes, soups, and stews.

Rye Flour Rye flour is quite heavy, and has a considerably stronger flavor than wheat. It doesn't rise too well, so in breads using yeast, the amount of yeast needed and the time needed for rising are about double what you would use for wheat flour.

Soy Flour Soy flour has a strong flavor but is a good combination flour. Soy flour contains more protein than other flours.

Tapioca Flour Tapioca flour blends well with other flours and is a good thickening agent.

Adapted from *Gluten Intolerance, revised edition*. © 1991, The American Dietetic Association. Used with permission.

Wheat-Free All-Purpose Flour Mixture

Ⓜ Ⓔ Ⓦ Ⓟ Ⓝ

1 cup cornstarch
2 cups rice flour

2 cups soy flour
3 cups potato starch flour

Use this mix in place of wheat flour in a recipe. Use slightly more flour mixture than recipe calls for. Reduce oven temperature by approximately 25° and bake a little longer. Store unused mixture in refrigerator or soy will become strong.

—Mary Jane Dykes

Breads and Breakfasts

✦✦

Our quick-bread recipes can be cooked as muffins or in individual loaf pans. Try including them in school lunches.

Bread machines are a wonder! If it's difficult to find commercially prepared bread, consider investing in one of these machines. They are simple to use—pour all ingredients in at once and press the start button. That's all there is to it! If your machine has a timer, you can combine the ingredients the night before and set the timer so you wake up in the morning to the smell of fresh bread.

Store wheat-free baked goods in the refrigerator and they won't crumble as easily.

Honey-Apple Pancakes

◆M◆E◆P◆S◆N◆

1 1/4 cups flour	2 tablespoons honey
2 teaspoons baking powder	1 tablespoon oil
1/4 teaspoon salt	1 1/2 tablespoons water, 1 1/2
1/8 teaspoon apple pie spice	tablespoons oil, 1 teaspoon
1/8 teaspoon baking soda	baking powder; mixed together
1/4 teaspoon cinnamon	1 apple, finely chopped
3/4 cup apple juice	

In a medium mixing bowl stir together flour, baking powder, salt, apple pie spice, baking soda, and cinnamon. In a small bowl stir together wet ingredients and chopped apple; add all at once to flour mixture, stirring until blended but still slightly lumpy. Let batter rest 2 to 3 minutes.

Pour the batter to form circles approximately 4 inches in diameter onto a hot, lightly greased griddle or heavy skillet. Cook for 2 to 3 minutes or until pancakes have a bubbly surface and slightly dry edges. Turn pancakes; cook for 2 to 3 minutes more or until golden brown. Makes about 8 4-inch pancakes.

—*Sue Carlsen*

Oat Pancakes

◆M◆E◆W◆P◆S◆N◆

1 cup quick oats	1 1/4 cups boiling water
3 tablespoons oil	1 tablespoon sugar

Preheat nonstick griddle. Mix ingredients together; stir until well blended. Let rest 3 to 5 minutes. Drop mixture onto hot griddle. Cook over medium heat. Flip pancakes when edges turn golden brown, about 5 to 7 minutes. Continue cooking for 2 to 3 minutes. Serve with applesauce or syrup.

Suggestion: Add coconut flakes or cocoa powder to the batter for variety.

Home-Style Pancakes

◆M◆E◆P◆S◆N◆

2 cups flour
4 teaspoons baking powder
1/2 teaspoon salt
2 tablespoons sugar

2 cups water
3 tablespoons oil
1/4 teaspoon vanilla extract

Sift dry ingredients together; add remaining ingredients and beat together. Pour the batter to form circles approximately 4 inches in diameter onto a hot, lightly greased griddle or heavy skillet. Cook for 2 to 3 minutes or until pancakes have a bubbly surface and slightly dry edges. Turn pancakes; cook for 2 to 3 minutes more or until golden brown.

Suggestions: For a special treat for the kids, pour batter onto a hot griddle in the shape of a teddy bear, Mickey Mouse, or bunny.

Add banana slices, blueberries, or other fruit to batter for variety.

Note: This batter can be used to make waffles.

Rice Flour Griddle Cakes

◆M◆E◆W◆P◆S◆N◆

1 cup rice flour
1 1/2 teaspoons baking powder
1/2 teaspoon salt
1 teaspoon sugar

1 1/2 tablespoons water, 1 1/2
   tablespoons oil, 1 teaspoon
   baking powder; combined
3/4 cup orange juice
1 tablespoon oil

Mix and then sift rice flour, baking powder, salt, and sugar. Mix wet ingredients together. Combine liquid ingredients with dry ingredients. Mix until just blended. Pour batter onto very hot griddle to make 5-inch cakes. Flip gently with a spatula after 2 to 3 minutes. Continue baking until golden brown.

Note: Griddle cakes may be wrapped and frozen. Reheat frozen griddle cakes in toaster or oven.

—Nancy Sanker

Banana-Rice Pancakes

◆M◆E◆W◆P◆S◆N◆

2 cups rice flour
1 tablespoon sugar
4 teaspoons baking powder
1 teaspoon salt
1 1/2 cups water

1/4 cup oil
4 1/2 tablespoons oil, 4 1/2 table-
    spoons water, 1 tablespoon
    baking powder; mixed together
1 banana, mashed

Preheat nonstick or greased griddle. Sift dry ingredients together. Combine remaining ingredients; add to dry ingredients, mixing just enough to blend together. Cook on hot griddle. Flip pancakes when edges turn slightly brown, and continue cooking until brown.

Note: Can be made without fruit.

Suggestion: Substitute apples or blueberries for banana.

Potato Pancakes

◆M◆E◆W◆P◆S◆N◆

1 cup cooked mashed potatoes
1 cup finely grated
    uncooked potatoes
1/2 teaspoon salt

1/2 teaspoon baking powder
2 tablespoons milk-free,
    soy-free margarine

Combine all the ingredients except margarine. Melt margarine in skillet over medium heat. Spoon the potato mixture into the skillet, forming pancakes, and cook until golden brown on the bottom; flip and continue cooking. Serve plain or with maple syrup. Makes 4 servings.

Note: Use bacon drippings instead of margarine to add flavor.

Orange-Flavored French Toast

◆M◆E◆P◆S◆N◆

1/4 cup orange juice
1/4 cup sugar
1 cup water
1/4 teaspoon vanilla extract

1/4 teaspoon cinnamon
milk-free sliced bread
confectioners sugar

Preheat greased or nonstick griddle. Mix together orange juice, sugar, water, vanilla, and cinnamon. Lay bread in wet mixture until well coated; turn and repeat. Cook on hot griddle. Turn once. Garnish with confectioners sugar.

Suggestion: Be creative—try this recipe with different fruit juices.

Hidden Surprise Muffins

◆M◆E◆P◆S◆N◆

1/2 cup milk-free, soy-free margarine
1 cup sugar
1 teaspoon vanilla extract
2 teaspoons baking powder
1/4 teaspoon salt
2 cups flour

1/2 cup water
3 tablespoons water, 3 tablespoons oil, 2 teaspoons baking powder; mixed together
about 4 tablespoons grape, raspberry, or strawberry jelly

Preheat oven to 375°. Line a muffin tin with paper liners. Beat the margarine and sugar until fluffy. Add remaining ingredients except jelly. Mix until just blended. Spoon the batter into the muffin cups until 1/3 full. Drop about 1 teaspoon of your favorite jelly into the center of the muffin cups and top with remaining batter. Bake for 25 to 30 minutes.

Note: If you use too much jelly, your muffins will look like erupted volcanoes!

Banana Muffins

◆M◆ ◆E◆ ◆W◆ ◆P◆ ◆S◆ ◆N◆

2 mashed bananas

1/3 cup sugar

1/4 cup oil

2 teaspoons baking powder

1/2 teaspoon vanilla extract

1 1/4 cups rice flour

1/2 teaspoon baking soda

Preheat oven to 325°. Line muffin tin with paper liners. Mix mashed banana, sugar, and oil together well. Add the baking powder, vanilla, rice flour, and baking soda; mix well. Pour into muffin cups and bake for 25 minutes or until done. Makes 12 muffins.

Cinnamuffins

◆M◆ ◆E◆ ◆P◆ ◆S◆ ◆N◆

1/4 cup oil

1/2 cup dark molasses

1 cup applesauce

1 1/2 cups flour

1/2 teaspoon baking soda

1 1/2 teaspoons baking powder

3/4 teaspoon cinnamon

1/2 teaspoon salt

1/2 cup raisins

Preheat oven to 375°. Line muffin tins with paper liners. Mix oil, molasses, and applesauce. Sift together the flour, baking soda, baking powder, cinnamon, and salt. Stir together wet and dry ingredients, then add raisins. Drop into muffin cups and bake for 18 to 20 minutes. Makes 12 small muffins or 8 to 10 large muffins.

Applesauce Muffins

◆M◆ ◆E◆ ◆P◆ ◆S◆ ◆N◆

1 1/4 cups applesauce

2 tablespoons oil

1/4 cup honey

1/4 cup sugar

1 packet Knox unflavored gelatin

2 tablespoons warm water

2 cups flour

2 teaspoons baking powder

3/4 teaspoon baking soda

1/2 teaspoon cinnamon

1/4 teaspoon nutmeg

Preheat oven to 375°. Line muffin tin with paper liners. In a large bowl, beat together the applesauce, oil, honey, and sugar. Soften gelatin in 2 tablespoons warm water (do not mix gelatin with water until you are ready to use or it will congeal). Add to applesauce mixture.

In a medium bowl, combine flour, baking powder, baking soda, cinnamon, and nutmeg. Add to applesauce mixture. Stir just enough to moisten dry ingredients. Pour into muffin cups. Bake for 20 minutes.

Suggestions: Top with 1/4 teaspoon cinnamon and 1/4 cup sugar, mixed together. Or add 3/4 cup chopped raisins.

Blueberry Muffins

Ⓜ Ⓔ Ⓟ Ⓢ Ⓝ

1/2 cup milk-free,
  soy-free margarine
  at room temperature
1 cup plus 2 tablespoons sugar
3 tablespoons water, 3 tablespoons oil,
  2 teaspoons baking powder;
  mixed together
1 teaspoon vanilla extract

2 teaspoons baking powder
1/4 teaspoon salt
2 cups flour
1/2 cup water
2 1/2 cups blueberries
1 tablespoon sugar mixed
  with 1/4 teaspoon ground
  nutmeg

Preheat oven to 375°. Line muffin tin with paper liners. In a medium-size bowl, beat margarine until creamy. Beat in the sugar until pale and fluffy. Beat in water, oil, and baking powder. Add vanilla, remaining baking powder, and salt.

Fold in half the flour and half the water with a spatula. Add remaining flour and water. Fold in blueberries. Scoop batter into muffin cups. Sprinkle with nutmeg-sugar. Bake 25 to 30 minutes or until golden brown. Let muffins cool slightly before serving.

Peach Breakfast Bread

◆M◆E◆P◆S◆N◆

1/2 cup canned peaches
1 cup sugar
2 tablespoons milk-free, soy-free
    margarine, melted
1 1/2 tablespoons oil, 1 1/2 tablespoons
    water, 1 teaspoon baking
    powder; mixed together

2 cups flour
1 tablespoon baking powder
1/2 teaspoon salt
1/4 teaspoon baking soda
1/2 cup orange juice
1/4 cup water

Preheat oven to 350°. Grease a 9x5x3-inch loaf pan. Drain and finely chop peaches; set aside. Beat sugar and margarine. Add oil, water, and baking powder mixture. Combine flour, baking powder, salt, and baking soda; add to creamed mixture. Add orange juice, then water, stirring after each addition. Stir in peaches.

Spoon mixture into loaf pan. Bake for 70 minutes or until a wooden pick inserted in center comes out clean. Cool in pan 10 minutes; remove from pan, and let cool on wire rack.

Suggestions: Add 1 cup chopped walnuts if allowed. Or use apricots instead of peaches.

Banana Bread

◆M◆E◆P◆S◆N◆

1/2 cup oil
1 cup sugar
3 tablespoons oil, 3 tablespoons water,
    2 teaspoons baking powder;
    mixed together

2 bananas, mashed
2 cups flour
1 tablespoon baking soda

Preheat oven to 350°. Grease and flour a 9x5-inch loaf pan. Mix all ingredients in the order given. Pour into pan and bake 40 to 50 minutes or until a wooden pick inserted in center comes out clean. Tastes great cooled or as toast.

Suggestion: Add 1/4 cup chopped nuts, if allowed.

Oat-Banana Bread

♦M♦ ♦E♦ ♦W♦ ♦P♦ ♦S♦ ♦N♦

2 1/2 cups oat flour
1 cup sugar
3 teaspoons baking soda

1/4 cup oil
1 cup apple juice
3 large bananas, mashed

Preheat oven to 350°. Mix all the ingredients together and pour into an 8x8-inch pan. Bake for 25 minutes or until done.

—Mary Beth Benko

Corn Muffins

♦M♦ ♦E♦ ♦W♦ ♦P♦ ♦S♦ ♦N♦

1/3 cup shortening
1/4 cup sugar
1 cup Cream of Rice cereal
1 tablespoon baking powder
2/3 cup warm water

1/4 teaspoon salt
1 teaspoon vanilla extract
1 teaspoon grated lemon rind
2/3 cup cornmeal
1/4 cup raisins, optional

Preheat oven to 375°. Line muffin tin with paper liners. Cream shortening and sugar. Mix rice cereal and baking powder in warm water. Combine with sugar and shortening mixture. Mix in remaining ingredients (and raisins, if used). Spoon into muffin cups (small muffins have a better texture). Bake 25 minutes. Makes 8 muffins.

Note: These muffins hold together better if you let them cool a few hours or overnight.

English Muffin Bread

◆M◆E◆P◆S◆N◆

6 cups flour
2 packages active dry yeast
1 tablespoon sugar
2 teaspoons salt

1/4 teaspoon baking soda
2 1/2 cups water
cornmeal

Grease two 8 1/2 x 4 1/2-inch pans and sprinkle with cornmeal. Combine 3 cups flour, yeast, sugar, salt, and baking soda; set aside. Heat water until very warm (120 to 130°). Add to dry mixture; beat well. Stir in rest of flour to make a stiff batter. Divide between two loaf pans. Sprinkle with cornmeal. Cover, and let rise in a warm place for 45 minutes.

Preheat oven to 400°. Bake for 25 minutes. Remove from pans immediately and cool on wire racks. It's best when sliced and toasted. This bread freezes well.

Zucchini Bread

◆M◆E◆P◆S◆N◆

3 cups flour
1/2 teaspoon baking powder
1 teaspoon salt
2 teaspoons cinnamon
1 teaspoon baking soda
2 cups grated zucchini (about
    3 medium zucchinis)

4 1/2 tablespoons water, 4 1/2 table-
    spoons oil, 1 tablespoon baking
    powder; mixed together
1 cup oil
3 teaspoons vanilla extract
2 cups sugar

Preheat oven to 350°. Sift together first 5 ingredients. Add the remaining ingredients and mix well. Pour into three loaf pans. Bake 55 minutes.

Note: This recipe freezes well.

Cinnamon Raisin Coffee Cake

◆M◆E◆P◆S◆N◆

1 cup plus 2 tablespoons water
2 cups raisins
1 cup brown sugar
1/3 cup milk-free,
    soy-free margarine
1/2 teaspoon cinnamon
1/2 teaspoon allspice

1/2 teaspoon salt
1/8 teaspoon nutmeg
2 cups sifted flour
1 teaspoon baking powder
1 teaspoon baking soda
Vanilla Icing (recipe below)

Preheat oven to 325°. Grease a 7-inch tube pan. In a medium saucepan, combine water, raisins, brown sugar, margarine, cinnamon, allspice, salt, and nutmeg; bring to a boil and cook for 3 minutes. Cool.

Sift flour before measuring, then sift again with baking powder and soda. Stir dry ingredients gradually into cooled mixture; beat with electric mixer until smooth. Turn into prepared tube pan and bake 35 minutes or until a cake tester comes out clean.

Drizzle with icing.

Vanilla Icing

◆M◆E◆W◆P◆S◆N◆

1 cup confectioners sugar
1 1/2 tablespoons warm water

1/4 teaspoon vanilla extract

Combine all ingredients and mix until smooth and silky.

Apple Rings

◆M◆E◆W◆P◆S◆N◆

2-3 apples
2 tablespoons milk-free, soy-free
   margarine, melted

2 teaspoons cinnamon mixed with
   1/4 cup sugar

Peel, core, and slice apples into rings. Sauté gently in margarine until golden brown and soft. Serve warm with cinnamon-sugar on top.

Suggestion: Coat apples with pancake batter and cook until golden. Serve with syrup.

Apple Coffee Cake

◆M◆E◆P◆S◆N◆

1/2 cup milk-free, soy-free
   margarine, softened
2 cups sugar
6 tablespoons water, 6 tablespoons oil,
   4 teaspoons baking powder;
   mixed together
2 cups flour

2 teaspoons baking powder
1/2 teaspoon salt
4 cups peeled and chopped
   apple (about 3 large apples)
1 teaspoon vanilla extract
1 1/2 tablespoons sugar
1/2 teaspoon ground cinnamon

Preheat oven to 350°. Grease and flour 13x9-inch pan. Beat margarine at medium speed with an electric mixer. Gradually add sugar; beat well. Add water, oil, and baking powder mixture.

In a separate bowl, combine flour, baking powder, and salt; add to creamed mixture. Stir in apple and vanilla. Spoon batter into greased and floured pan. Combine remaining sugar and cinnamon; sprinkle over cake batter. Bake for 45 minutes or until a wooden pick inserted in center comes out clean. Serve warm or cool. Yield: 15 servings.

Orange Glaze

Ⓜ Ⓔ Ⓦ Ⓟ Ⓢ Ⓝ

1/2 cup confectioners sugar

4 teaspoons orange juice

Mix ingredients until smooth. Add enough juice to produce an easy-to-pour mixture.

Caramel Glaze

Ⓜ Ⓔ Ⓦ Ⓟ Ⓢ Ⓝ

3 tablespoons packed brown sugar
2 tablespoons dark corn syrup

3 tablespoons milk-free, soy-free
   margarine

In a small saucepan, combine ingredients. Bring to boil over medium heat. Continue cooking until brown sugar is completely dissolved. Remove from heat and let mixture cool a bit before drizzling over muffins or bread.

Cinnamon Topping

Ⓜ Ⓔ Ⓦ Ⓟ Ⓢ Ⓝ

1/4 cup sugar
2 teaspoons ground cinnamon

1 tablespoon milk-free, soy-free
   margarine, melted

Mix all ingredients and sprinkle over hot muffins.

Honey Glaze

Ⓜ Ⓔ Ⓦ Ⓟ Ⓢ Ⓝ

1/4 cup honey
2 tablespoons sugar

1 tablespoon milk-free, soy-free
   margarine

In a saucepan, combine ingredients. Bring to a boil over medium heat, stirring continuously. Remove from heat, and let cool slightly (keep warm). Drizzle over bread or muffins.

Vanilla Icing

◆M◆E◆W◆P◆S◆N◆

1 cup confectioners sugar   1/4 teaspoon vanilla extract
1 1/2 tablespoons water

Mix all ingredients at once. Drizzle over muffins or bread.

Note: Lemon extract may be substituted for the vanilla extract.

Poppy or Sesame Topping for Baked Breads

◆M◆E◆W◆P◆S◆N◆

warm water   poppy seeds or sesame seeds

Before cooking, brush bread or biscuit dough with warm water; sprinkle with poppy or sesame seeds.

Apple Muffins with Brown Sugar Sauce

◆M◆E◆P◆S◆N◆

1 cup brown sugar, firmly packed   2 tablespoons boiling water
1 cup flour   1 tablespoon milk-free, soy-free
1 cup apples, peeled and   margarine, melted
   diced   1 teaspoon baking soda
1 1/2 tablespoons water, 1 1/2 table-   1 teaspoon vanilla extract
   spoons oil, 1 teaspoon baking   1/8 teaspoon salt
   powder; mixed together   Brown Sugar Sauce (see page 27)

Preheat oven to 350°. Line muffin tin with paper liners. Combine all ingredients except Brown Sugar Sauce in a large bowl. Stir until well blended. Fill muffin tins 2/3 full. Bake 25 minutes or until a cake tester inserted in center comes out clean. Pour Brown Sugar Sauce over muffins while sauce is hot.

Brown Sugar Sauce

◆M◆E◆W◆P◆S◆N◆

1 cup brown sugar
2 tablespoons cornstarch
1/2 cup boiling water

4 tablespoons milk-free, soy-free
    margarine, melted
1 teaspoon vanilla extract

Mix brown sugar and cornstarch in small saucepan. Add water, margarine, and vanilla extract. Cook over medium-low heat until thickened.

Cinnamon Biscuits

◆M◆E◆P◆S◆N◆

2 cups flour
2 teaspoons baking powder
1 1/2 tablespoons sugar
1/2 teaspoon cinnamon
1/4 teaspoon salt

3 tablespoons milk-free, soy-free
    margarine, cut into small pieces
1/2 cup raisins
3/4 cup water
Topping (recipe below)

Preheat oven to 450°. In large bowl, combine flour, baking powder, sugar, cinnamon, and salt. Cut in margarine with a fork until mixture resembles coarse oatmeal. Add raisins. Mix well. Add water and stir until all ingredients are moistened. On a floured surface, knead dough 2 minutes. Roll to 1/4-inch thickness. Cut with biscuit cutter or top of a glass. Place on a baking sheet. Bake for 11 minutes or until golden.

Topping

1/2 cup confectioners sugar

1 tablespoon water

Combine sugar and water. Stir well. Drizzle over biscuits while they are still warm.

Golden Brown Muffins

1 3/4 cups flour
1/3 cup sugar
2 1/2 teaspoons baking powder
1/2 teaspoon salt
1/2 teaspoon ground cinnamon
1/8 teaspoon baking soda

1 1/2 tablespoons oil, 1 1/2 table-
    spoons water, 1 teaspoon baking
    powder; mixed together
3/4 cup apple juice
1/3 cup oil

Preheat oven to 400°. Line muffin tin with paper liners. In a large mixing bowl, stir together flour, sugar, baking powder, salt, cinnamon, and baking soda. Set aside. In a small mixing bowl stir together oil, water, and baking powder mixture; apple juice; and oil. Pour wet mixture into flour mixture. Stir together well. Fill prepared muffin tins 2/3 full. Bake 18 minutes or until golden brown. Serve warm.

Sweet Oatmeal Muffins

1 1/2 cups quick oats
1 cup flour
2 teaspoons baking powder
1/2 teaspoon salt
1 cup dark brown sugar,
    firmly packed

3 tablespoons oil, 3 tablespoons
    water, 2 teaspoons baking
    powder; mixed together
3/4 cup water
1/4 cup oil
1 teaspoon vanilla extract

Preheat oven to 400°. Line muffin tin with paper liners. In a large bowl, mix oats, flour, baking powder, and salt. Set aside. In another bowl, combine brown sugar and oil, water, and baking powder mixture until smooth. Add water, oil, and vanilla extract. Pour over dry ingredients and mix gently until well blended. Pour batter into prepared muffin tins. Bake 15 to 20 minutes or until a cake tester inserted in center comes out clean. Remove and place on wire rack to cool.

Chocolate Pancakes

◆M◆◆E◆◆P◆◆S◆◆N◆

2 cups flour	1/2 teaspoon salt
3 tablespoons sugar	2 1/4 cups water
2 tablespoons unsweetened cocoa powder	3 tablespoons oil
4 teaspoons baking powder	Strawberry Sauce (recipe below)

In a large bowl, mix flour, sugar, cocoa, baking powder, and salt. Add water and oil, and stir until batter is completely blended. If the batter is too stiff, add a little more water. Let the batter stand several minutes. Preheat griddle. Prepare Strawberry Sauce. Set aside. Pour pancake batter onto hot griddle; flip pancakes when bubbles appear on top. Remove to plates and top with Strawberry Sauce.

Strawberry Sauce

◆M◆◆E◆◆W◆◆P◆◆S◆◆N◆

1/3 cup sugar	3 tablespoons strawberry preserves
1/2 cup water	1/2 cup fresh strawberries, halved

Pour all ingredients into small saucepan. Cook over medium-low heat, stirring constantly. Bring to a slow boil, then remove from heat. Spoon over warm pancakes.

Apple Crunch Muffins

◆M◆E◆P◆S◆N◆

3 cups flour	2 teaspoons baking powder
1 1/2 cups brown sugar, firmly packed	1/2 teaspoon baking soda
1/2 teaspoon salt	2 teaspoons baking powder,
2 teaspoons cinnamon, divided	2 tablespoons water,
1 teaspoon ground ginger	2 tablespoons vinegar;
2/3 cup shortening	mixed together
1/2 cup quick oats	1 cup apple juice

Preheat oven to 375°. Line muffin tin with paper liners. Stir together flour, brown sugar, salt, 1 teaspoon of cinnamon, and ginger. Add shortening; mix until crumbly. Put 2/3 cup of mixture in small bowl and mix in oats and remaining teaspoon of cinnamon. Set aside. Add baking powder; baking soda; and baking powder, water, and vinegar mixture to remaining mixture. Mix well. Add apple juice and stir until well blended. Fill each muffin cup 2/3 full. Top with oat mixture. Bake 15 to 20 minutes or until a cake tester inserted in center comes out clean.

Apples and Cornflakes

◆M◆E◆W◆P◆S◆N◆

3 tablespoons sugar	1 cup cornflakes
1/4 teaspoon cinnamon	1/2 cup water
6 apples	
6 tablespoons milk-free, soy-free margarine	

Preheat oven to 350°. Mix together sugar and cinnamon; set aside. Peel and thinly slice apples. Set aside. Grease casserole dish. Arrange one layer of apples in dish. Sprinkle with sugar and cinnamon; dot with margarine. Cover with a layer of cornflakes. Repeat layering until all apples are used. Pour water over top. Cover and bake 45 minutes.

Suggestion: This recipe is delicious as a hot breakfast or as a side dish to a main meal.

Honey Breakfast Bread

◆M◆E◆P◆S◆N◆

1 cup water
1 cup honey
1/2 cup sugar
2 1/2 cups flour
1 teaspoon baking soda
1 teaspoon salt

1/4 cup milk-free, soy-free
  margarine, melted
3 tablespoons water, 3 tablespoons
  oil, 2 teaspoons baking powder;
  mixed together

Preheat oven to 325°. Grease and flour a loaf pan; set aside. Pour water into a medium saucepan and bring to a simmer over medium heat. Add honey and sugar. Stir until the sugar is dissolved. Set aside until cooled.

In a medium bowl, stir together flour, baking soda, and salt. Set aside. Add the melted margarine and the water, oil, and baking powder mixture to the cooled honey mixture. Stir until well mixed. Combine with dry ingredients. Beat until thoroughly blended. Pour into prepared pan. Bake 75 minutes or until a cake tester inserted in center comes out clean. Cool in the pan. Remove to a wire rack and let cool completely.

Fried Ripe Bananas

◆M◆E◆W◆P◆S◆N◆

1 banana
1 cup barley flour
1 cup water
1 tablespoon sugar

1/8 teaspoon cinnamon
2 tablespoons milk-free,
  soy-free margarine
1/4 cup sugar

Cut the banana into 1/4-inch slices. Set aside. In an airtight container mix together flour, water, sugar, and cinnamon. Add banana slices. Cover and shake gently until the bananas are well coated. Set aside. Melt margarine in a frying pan; add the bananas and fry until browned. Gently turn bananas once. Remove from pan, roll in sugar, and serve.

Suggestion: Serve with hot cereal for breakfast or as a dessert.

—*Valerie Floccare*

Chocolate-Banana Muffins

◆M◆E◆P◆S◆N◆

1/2 cup milk-free, soy-free margarine	2 teaspoons baking powder
1 cup sugar	1/4 teaspoon salt
3 tablespoons water, 3 tablespoons oil,	1/4 cup unsweetened cocoa powder
2 teaspoons baking powder; mixed	1 banana, mashed
together	2 cups flour, divided
1 teaspoon vanilla extract	1/2 cup water, divided

Preheat oven to 375°. Line muffin tin with paper liners. In a medium bowl, beat margarine until creamy. Beat in sugar until pale and fluffy. Add water, oil, and baking powder mixture, and mix well. Beat in vanilla extract, baking powder, salt, and cocoa powder. Add mashed banana, and stir well. Fold in half the flour with a spatula, then add half the water. Repeat with remaining flour and water. Mix well.

Scoop batter into prepared muffin tins. Bake 25 to 30 minutes, or until a cake tester inserted in center comes out clean. Let muffins cool at least 30 minutes in pan before removing.

Suggestion: These muffins can be served for breakfast or as a lunchtime treat.

Crunchy Breakfast Bread

◆M◆E◆P◆S◆N◆

1 3/4 cups flour	2 tablespoons grated orange rind
2 1/2 teaspoons baking powder	1 1/2 tablespoons water, 1 1/2 table-
1/2 teaspoon salt	spoons oil, 1 teaspoon baking
1 cup sugar	powder; mixed together
3/4 cup cornflakes	1 cup water
1/2 cup raisins	1/4 cup oil

Preheat oven to 350°. Grease and flour an 8 1/2 x 4 1/2 x 3-inch loaf pan. In a large bowl, combine flour, baking powder, salt, sugar, cereal, raisins, and orange rind. Set aside. In another bowl, combine water, oil, and baking powder mixture; water; and oil. Stir well. Add to dry ingredients; stir mixture until just moistened. Pour into prepared loaf pan. Bake 1 hour or until a cake tester inserted in center comes out clean. Cool 10 minutes on a wire rack, remove from pan to wire rack, and let cool completely before serving.

Baking Powder Biscuits

◆M◆ ◆E◆ ◆P◆ ◆S◆ ◆N◆

2 cups flour	1 teaspoon salt
1 tablespoon sugar	1/3 cup oil
1 tablespoon baking powder	2/3 cup water

Preheat oven to 450°. Mix together the flour, sugar, baking powder, and salt. Set aside. In another bowl, mix the oil and water together. Add them to the dry mixture until it is moist. Add more water, if necessary, to make dough soft, but not too sticky. Knead dough 20 to 25 times on a floured board. Roll or pat the dough to 1/2-inch thickness. Cut it into circles. Place on an ungreased cookie sheet. Bake 10 to 12 minutes or until the tops are golden brown.

—Nancy Woo Walker

Rye Muffins

◆M◆ ◆E◆ ◆W◆ ◆P◆ ◆S◆ ◆N◆

1 1/4 cups rye flour	1/4 cup sugar
1/2 cup rice flour	1 cup water
4 teaspoons baking powder	1/4 cup oil
3/4 teaspoon salt	

Preheat oven to 375°. Line muffin tin with paper liners. In a large bowl, mix flours, baking powder, salt, and sugar together. Add water and oil. Blend well. Fill muffin tins about 3/4 full. Bake 25 minutes or until a cake tester inserted in center comes out clean.

Pear Muffins

◆M◆◆E◆◆P◆◆S◆◆N◆

2 cups flour
1 3/4 teaspoons baking powder
3/4 teaspoon baking soda
1/4 teaspoon salt
1 1/2 teaspoons ground ginger
1/2 teaspoon freshly grated nutmeg
1/4 teaspoon ground allspice
7 tablespoons milk-free,
　soy-free margarine,
　melted and cooled

2/3 cup light brown sugar, firmly
　packed
2 tablespoons sugar
1 1/2 tablespoons water, 1 1/2 table-
　spoons oil, 1 teaspoon baking
　powder; mixed together
1 1/2 teaspoons vanilla extract
1/2 cup water
1 1/4 cups canned or ripe pears,
　cut up

Preheat oven to 400°. Line muffin tin with paper liners. Sift together flour, baking powder, baking soda, salt, ginger, nutmeg, and allspice; set aside. In a large bowl, whisk together margarine and sugars until fluffy. Add water, oil, and baking powder mixture; vanilla extract; and water. Combine with flour mixture and stir until well blended. Stir in pears. Pour batter into prepared muffin cups. Bake 17 to 20 minutes, or until a cake tester inserted into middle comes out clean.

Note: Add 1/4 cup raisins for variety.

Blueberry Corn Muffins

◆M◆◆E◆◆W◆◆P◆◆S◆◆N◆

1/3 cup shortening	1/4 teaspoon salt
1/4 cup sugar	2 teaspoons vanilla extract
1 cup Cream of Rice cereal	2/3 cup cornmeal
1 tablespoon baking powder	3/4 cup blueberries
2/3 cup warm water	

Preheat oven to 375°. Line muffin tin with paper liners. Cream shortening and sugar; set aside. In another bowl, mix rice cereal and baking powder in warm water. Combine with shortening and sugar mixture. Mix in remaining ingredients. Spoon mixture into muffin cups. Bake 25 minutes.

Note: These muffins hold together better if you let them cool a few hours or overnight.

Zesty Zucchini Muffins

◆M◆◆E◆◆P◆◆S◆◆N◆

2 cups flour	3/4 cup water
1/2 cup sugar	3 tablespoons oil
1 tablespoon baking powder	1 cup zucchini, coarsely shredded
2 teaspoons grated lemon rind	1 1/2 tablespoons water, 1 1/2 table-
1/4 teaspoon salt	spoons oil, 1 teaspoon baking
1/4 teaspoon ground nutmeg	powder; mixed together

Preheat oven to 400°. Line muffin tin with paper liners. Combine dry ingredients in a bowl; set aside. Combine water, oil, and zucchini. Add water, oil, and baking powder mixture; stir well. Combine with flour mixture, stirring until dry ingredients are moistened. Pour into muffin cups. Bake 20 minutes or until golden. Let cool on a wire rack.

Suggestion: These muffins can be served for breakfast, lunch, or dinner.

Apple-Raisin Bread

◆M◆E◆P◆S◆N◆

4 cups flour	2 teaspoons baking powder,
1 3/4 cups sugar	2 tablespoons water, 2 table-
1 tablespoon baking powder	spoons vinegar; mixed together
1 1/2 teaspoons salt	1 1/2 cups apple juice
1 teaspoon baking soda	2 cups raisins
1/2 cup milk-free, soy-free margarine	3 apples, peeled, cored, and diced

Preheat oven to 350°. Grease and flour two loaf pans. Mix flour, sugar, baking powder, salt, and baking soda. Cut in margarine until mixture resembles coarse crumbs. Set aside. Mix baking powder, water, and vinegar mixture with apple juice. Stir juice mixture into flour mixture until moistened. Fold in raisins and apples. Spoon into loaf pans. Bake 1 hour, or until cake tester inserted in center comes out clean. Cool breads 10 minutes on wire rack. Remove from pans.

—Linda Borschuk

David's Favorite French Bread

◆M◆E◆P◆S◆N◆

3/4 cup warm water	1 tablespoon milk-free, soy-free margarine
1 teaspoon salt	2 cups flour
1 tablespoon sugar	1 1/2 teaspoons yeast

To make a 1-lb. loaf: Pour warm water (70–80°, a little warm to the touch), salt, sugar, and margarine into the bread machine. Add flour and make a small indentation in flour for yeast. Pour in yeast. Close top and set machine to French-bread setting. (Most machines have this setting.) When done, shake loaf out of machine and let cool on rack.

Note: Bread machines may vary regarding order of ingredients. Follow your own machine manufacturer's recommendations.

—Susan Leavitt

Banana-Honey Muffins

◆M◆E◆P◆S◆N◆

3/4 cup mashed ripe bananas
(about 2 medium bananas)
1/2 cup water
1 teaspoon baking powder, 1 tablespoon
water, 1 tablespoon vinegar,
mixed together
3 tablespoons honey

3 tablespoons oil
1 1/4 cups flour
2 1/4 teaspoons baking powder
1/4 teaspoon salt
1 1/4 cups Total cereal, slightly
crushed
Streusel Topping (recipe below)

Preheat oven to 400°. Line muffin tin with paper liners. In a large bowl, mix bananas; water; baking powder, water, and vinegar mixture; honey; and oil. Stir in flour, baking powder, and salt until just moistened. Stir in cereal. Fill each muffin cup about 2/3 full.

Streusel Topping

1 tablespoon brown sugar, firmly packed
1 tablespoon milk-free, soy-free
margarine, softened

1 tablespoon flour
1/3 cup crushed Total cereal

Combine all ingredients for streusel topping. Sprinkle streusel evenly over muffins. Bake about 20 minutes or until golden brown. Serve with jelly.

—Linda Borschuk

Oatmeal-Raisin Loaf

◆M◆E◆P◆S◆N◆

1 1/4 cups apple juice
1/2 cup uncooked quick oats
1 1/2 cups flour
1 teaspoon ground cinnamon
1 teaspoon ground ginger
1 teaspoon baking soda
1 teaspoon baking powder
1/2 teaspoon salt

1/2 cup sugar
1/2 cup milk-free, soy-free
margarine, melted
3 tablespoons water, 3 tablespoons
oil, 2 teaspoons baking powder;
mixed together
1/2 cup raisins

In a large bowl, stir together apple juice and oats. Let stand 30 minutes. Preheat the oven to 350°. Grease and flour a medium loaf pan. Set aside. In a small bowl, stir together flour, cinnamon, ginger, baking soda, baking powder, and salt. Set aside. Combine sugar and margarine with the water, oil, and baking powder mixture. Stir in raisins. Add to oatmeal mixture. Stir well. Combine with dry ingredients; stir until well blended.

Pour batter evenly into prepared pan. Bake 1 hour or until a thin wooden skewer inserted in the center of the loaf comes out clean. Cool in the pan 10 minutes; remove to wire rack to cool completely.

Raisin Bread

◆M◆E◆P◆S◆N◆

2 cups light brown sugar, firmly packed	1 teaspoon salt
2 cups water	1 teaspoon cinnamon
15-ounce package raisins	1/4 teaspoon ground cloves
2 tablespoons milk-free, soy-free margarine	3 cups flour
	1 teaspoon baking soda

In a 3-quart saucepan, combine brown sugar, water, raisins, margarine, salt, cinnamon, and cloves. Bring to boil over medium heat. Reduce heat and simmer 5 minutes. Let cool, then refrigerate until thickened and chilled, about 2 hours. Stir occasionally.

Preheat oven to 325°. Grease and flour two 8 1/2 x 4 1/2-inch loaf pans. Set aside. In a large bowl, mix flour, baking soda, and chilled mixture until flour is thoroughly moistened. Divide batter between loaf pans. Bake 1 hour and 10 minutes or until a cake tester inserted in center comes out clean. Cool in pans 10 minutes. Remove from pans to cool completely.

Raspberry Cinnamon Muffins

Ⓜ Ⓔ Ⓟ Ⓢ Ⓝ

1 1/2 cups flour
1/2 cup sugar
2 1/2 teaspoons baking powder
1 teaspoon ground cinnamon
1/4 teaspoon salt
2/3 cup water
1/4 cup milk-free, soy-free margarine, melted

1 1/2 tablespoons water, 1 1/2 tablespoons oil, 1 teaspoon baking powder; mixed together
1/4 cup raspberry preserves
1 tablespoon sugar
1/4 teaspoon ground cinnamon

Preheat oven to 400°. Line muffin tin with paper liners. Set aside. In a medium bowl, combine flour, sugar, baking powder, cinnamon, and salt. Set aside. In another bowl, combine water and margarine. Add water, oil, and baking powder mixture. Stir well. Add to the flour mixture; blend well. Spoon batter into muffin cups until 1/3 full. Spoon 1 teaspoon preserves into center of each muffin cup and top with remaining batter.

Combine 1 tablespoon sugar and 1/4 teaspoon cinnamon; stir well. Sprinkle evenly over muffins. Bake 20 minutes or until cake tester inserted into middle comes out clean. Cool muffins on a wire rack.

Carrot Breakfast Muffins

Ⓜ Ⓔ Ⓟ Ⓢ Ⓝ

1 3/4 cups flour
2 teaspoons baking powder
1/2 teaspoon salt
1/2 cup grated carrots
1/2 cup water

1 1/2 tablespoons water, 1 1/2 tablespoons oil, 1 teaspoon baking powder; mixed together
1/3 cup oil
1/4 cup honey

Preheat oven to 400°. Line muffin tin with paper liners. Set aside. In a large bowl, stir together flour, baking powder, and salt. Set aside. In a medium bowl, mix together carrots; water; water, oil, and baking powder mixture; oil; and honey. Add to dry ingredients. Stir. Fill muffin tins 2/3 full. Bake 20 minutes, or until golden brown.

Sticky Muffins

◆M◆E◆P◆S◆N◆

6 tablespoons packed brown sugar	1/2 teaspoon salt
1 cup drained, canned unsweetened pineapple chunks	3/4 cup water
	3/4 cup maple syrup
1 3/4 cups flour	1/4 cup cooking oil
1 teaspoon baking powder	2 tablespoons vanilla extract
1/2 teaspoon baking soda	1 tablespoon lemon juice

Preheat oven to 350°. Line muffin tin with paper liners. Set aside. Place 1 tablespoon brown sugar and 1 layer pineapple chunks in the bottom of each muffin cup; set aside. Combine flour, baking powder, baking soda, and salt. Set aside. Combine water, maple syrup, oil, vanilla extract, and lemon juice; stir well. Add to flour mixture, stirring just until moistened. Divide cake batter evenly into muffin cups. Bake 30 minutes, or until a wooden pick inserted in center of muffins comes out clean. Invert muffins onto a wire rack. Serve warm or at room temperature.

Healthy Breakfast Muffins

◆M◆E◆P◆S◆N◆

1 cup whole wheat flour	1 1/2 tablespoons water, 1 1/2 table-
1 cup quick-cooking oats	spoons oil, 1 teaspoon baking
2 1/2 teaspoons baking powder	powder; mixed together
1/2 teaspoon baking soda	3/4 cup water
1/2 teaspoon salt	1/3 cup oil
1/4 cup brown sugar, firmly packed	

Preheat oven to 400°. Line muffin tin with paper liners. Set aside. In large bowl, stir together flour, oats, baking powder, baking soda, salt, and brown sugar. Set aside. In small bowl, mix together water, oil, and baking powder mixture with water and oil. Stir well. Add to dry ingredients. Stir until moistened. Fill muffin tins 2/3 full. Bake 20 minutes or until golden brown. Serve with warm jam or jelly.

Moist Halloween Muffins

◆Ⓜ◆Ⓔ◆Ⓟ◆Ⓢ◆Ⓝ◆

1 1/2 cups flour
2/3 cup sugar
1/4 cup brown sugar, firmly packed
2 teaspoons baking powder
3/4 teaspoon salt
1/2 teaspoon cinnamon
1/2 teaspoon nutmeg
1 1/2 tablespoons oil, 1 1/2 tablespoons water, 1 teaspoon baking
   powder; mixed together

8-ounce can crushed pineapple,
   drained
1/2 cup canned pumpkin
1/2 cup water
1/4 cup milk-free, soy-free
   margarine, melted

Preheat oven to 425°. Line muffin tin with paper liners decorated for Halloween. Set aside. In a large bowl, mix together flour, sugars, baking powder, salt, cinnamon, and nutmeg. Set aside. In another bowl, mix together oil, water, and baking powder mixture; pineapple; pumpkin; water; and margarine. Combine with dry ingredients and mix well. Batter will be stiff. Spoon into muffin tins, filling each 2/3 full. Bake 20 minutes or until golden brown. Cool on wire racks. Serve plain or frosted.

Note: For a Halloween celebration, let children decorate muffins with allowed candies, including candy corn, licorice, and candy pumpkins.

Cinnamon Swirl Coffee Cake

◆M◆E◆P◆S◆N◆

1/3 cup brown sugar, firmly packed
3 tablespoons flour
1 tablespoon cinnamon
1 1/4 cups confectioners sugar
1/3 cup oil
3 tablespoons water, 3 tablespoons oil,
  2 teaspoons baking powder; mixed
  together

3 cups flour
1 teaspoon baking powder
1 teaspoon baking soda
1/2 teaspoon salt
1 1/2 cups water
1 tablespoon vanilla extract

Preheat oven to 350°. Grease a Bundt pan. Set aside. In a small bowl, combine brown sugar, flour, and cinnamon. Stir well. Sprinkle 1/3 cup cinnamon mixture into pan. Set aside. In a large bowl, combine sugar and oil. Mix thoroughly. Add water, oil, and baking powder mixture. Beat well and set aside.

In a separate bowl, sift together flour, baking powder, baking soda, and salt. Add to creamed mixture alternately with remaining 1 1/2 cups water. Stir in vanilla extract. Measure 2 cups of batter; set aside. Pour remaining batter into prepared pan; sprinkle with cinnamon mixture. Pour reserved 2 cups batter over cinnamon mixture. Bake 45 minutes or until wooden pick inserted in center comes out clean. Cool in pan 10 minutes. Transfer to wire rack to cool completely.

Apple Pie Muffins

◆M◆E◆P◆S◆N◆

2 cups flour
2/3 cup sugar
1 tablespoon baking powder
1/2 teaspoon salt
2 teaspoons apple pie spice

1 1/2 tablespoons water, 1 1/2 tablespoons oil, 1 teaspoon baking
  powder; mixed together
1 1/2 cups water
1/3 cup milk-free, soy-free
  margarine, melted

Preheat oven to 400°. Line muffin tin with paper liners and set aside. In a large bowl, stir together flour, sugar, baking powder, salt, and apple pie spice. Set aside. In a medium bowl, mix together water, oil, and baking powder mixture, water, and margarine. Add to combined dry ingredients and stir until just blended. Spoon into prepared muffin tins. Bake 20 minutes, or until a wooden pick inserted in the center comes out clean. Cool 5 minutes in muffin tins before serving.

Almost French Crepes

M E W P S N

1/4 cup oat flour	1 1/2 tablespoons water, 1 1/2 table-
1/4 cup rice flour	spoons oil, 1 teaspoon baking
1 tablespoon sugar	powder; mixed together
1/8 teaspoon salt	6 tablespoons apricot preserves
3/4 cup water	1 1/2 teaspoons powdered sugar

In a medium bowl, combine flours, sugar, salt, water, and water, oil, and baking powder mixture. Set aside. Coat a 10-inch nonstick skillet with cooking spray, and place over medium-high heat until hot. Remove pan from heat, and pour 1/4 cup batter into pan; quickly tilt pan in all directions so batter covers pan with a thin film. Cook about 1 minute. Lift edge of crepe carefully with a spatula to test for doneness. Flip and cook an additional 30 seconds or until light golden color. Remove to plate.

Spread 1 tablespoon preserves over entire pancake, and roll up. Sprinkle with powdered sugar. Repeat with remaining batter.

Note: May be used for dessert or breakfast. Substitute your favorite preserves or fruit.

Pear Coffee Cake
◆M◆E◆P◆S◆N◆

1/2 cup milk-free, soy-free margarine, softened
1/2 cup sugar
4 1/2 tablespoons water, 4 1/2 tablespoons oil, 1 tablespoon baking powder; mixed together

1 cup flour
1/4 teaspoon salt
4 large canned pears, cut into slices
2 tablespoons sugar
freshly grated nutmeg

Preheat oven to 350°. Grease a 9x12-inch baking pan. Set aside. In a mixing bowl, beat together margarine and 1/2 cup sugar until light and fluffy. Add water, oil, and baking powder mixture. Mix thoroughly. Stir in flour and salt; beat until well blended. Spoon batter into prepared baking dish. Arrange pear slices in rows on top of batter. Sprinkle with remaining sugar and dust with nutmeg. Bake 55 minutes or until golden brown. Cool on wire rack.

Note: This is great for breakfast or as a warm dessert.

Apple Crisp
◆M◆E◆P◆S◆N◆

6 to 8 medium Granny Smith apples, peeled and sliced
1/2 cup brown sugar

2 tablespoons flour
1/4 cup water
1 teaspoon cinnamon

Preheat oven to 350°. Grease a 9x11-inch casserole dish, set aside. In a large bowl, mix above ingredients together. Arrange in layers in prepared dish.

Crumb Topping
1 1/2 cups brown sugar
1 cup flour

1/2 cup milk-free, soy-free margarine

In medium bowl, combine all ingredients. Mix until crumbly. Sprinkle on top of sliced apple mixture. Bake 30 minutes or until apples are soft.

—Leslie Price

Breakfast Puffs

◆M◆◆E◆◆P◆◆S◆◆N◆

1/3 cup milk-free, soy-free margarine, melted

1/2 cup sugar

1 1/2 tablespoons water, 1 1/2 tablespoons oil, 1 teaspoon baking powder; mixed together

1 1/2 cups flour

1 1/2 teaspoons baking powder

1/2 teaspoon salt

1/4 teaspoon ground nutmeg

1/2 cup water

1/4 cup sugar

1/2 teaspoon ground cinnamon

2 tablespoons milk-free, soy-free margarine, melted

Preheat oven to 350°. Grease miniature (1 3/4-inch) muffin tins and set aside. In mixing bowl, blend margarine, sugar, and water, oil, and baking powder mixture until creamy. Set aside. In another bowl, combine flour, baking powder, salt, and nutmeg. Combine flour mixture, margarine mixture, and water. Blend well. Fill prepared muffin tins 2/3 full. Bake 16 to 18 minutes. Remove from pans. Combine sugar and cinnamon. Dip tops of muffins in melted margarine, then in sugar mixture.

Bread Bowls

◆M◆◆E◆◆P◆◆S◆◆N◆

1/3 cup milk-free, soy-free margarine

3 cups self-rising flour

1 cup water

cornmeal

Preheat oven to 425°. In a blender, cut margarine into flour until crumbly. Add water and stir until moistened. Turn dough out onto a lightly floured surface. Knead a few times. Add more flour if dough is too sticky to handle. Grease the outside of an inverted ovenproof bowl. Sprinkle with cornmeal. Mold dough around the outside of bowl, cutting away excess. Place bowl on oven rack, open end down. Bake 17 minutes. Separate bread from bowl while still warm to avoid sticking. Fill with vegetables or fruits.

Note: Baking time may vary depending on bowl size.

Streusel-Oat Scones

◆M◆E◆P◆S◆N◆

2 cups flour
1/4 cup sugar
2 teaspoons baking powder
1/4 teaspoon baking soda
1/4 teaspoon salt

1/4 cup milk-free, soy-free margarine, chilled and cut into pieces
3/4 cup water
Scone Topping (recipe below)

Preheat oven to 450°. Grease a baking sheet and set aside. In a medium bowl, combine flour, sugar, baking powder, baking soda, and salt. Cut in margarine with a pastry blender until crumbly. Add water until mixture is moist. Place dough on prepared baking sheet and pat into 8-inch circle. Set aside.

Scone Topping

1/4 cup quick-cooking oats
1/4 cup brown sugar, firmly packed

1 tablespoon milk-free, soy-free margarine, melted
1 tablespoon flour

To prepare topping, in a small bowl, combine oats, brown sugar, margarine, and flour. Pat mixture into surface of rounded dough. Cut dough into 12 wedges, but do not separate the wedges. Bake 15 minutes or until lightly browned. Serve warm.

Cranberry Bread

◆M◆E◆P◆S◆N◆

2 cups flour
2 teaspoons baking powder
1/4 teaspoon salt (optional)
3 tablespoons oil
1 1/2 teaspoons grated orange peel
1 cup dried cranberries

1 1/2 tablespoons water, 1 1/2 tablespoons oil, 1 teaspoon baking powder; mixed together
1/2 cup orange juice
3/4 cup maple syrup

Preheat oven to 350°. Lightly grease and flour a 2-quart loaf pan; set aside. In a large bowl, sift together flour, baking powder, and salt. Drizzle oil over dry ingredients. Stir briefly with a wooden spoon. Mixture will look dry. Add orange peel and cranberries; stir to coat with flour mixture. Set aside. In a separate bowl, mix water, oil, and baking powder mixture, juice, and syrup. Combine contents of the two bowls; mix just enough to incorporate flour. Batter will be stiff.

Spoon into prepared loaf pan. Bake 1 hour or until loaf is well risen and a cake tester inserted in the center comes out clean. Remove bread from pan. Cool on wire rack before serving.

Pumpkin Doughnuts

4 1/2 cups flour	1 1/4 cups nondairy creamer*
4 teaspoons baking powder	1 teaspoon yeast in 1/4 cup warm water
3/4 teaspoon salt	3/4 cup cooked mashed pumpkin
1 cup sugar	1/2 cup sugar
1 teaspoon nutmeg	1/2 teaspoon cinnamon

In large bowl, combine all ingredients up to and including pumpkin and stir until just blended. Roll dough on well-floured board to 1/4-inch thickness. Cut with doughnut cutter. Fry in deep, hot fat (about 375°) until golden brown on one side; turn and fry until brown on the other side. Drain on a clean brown paper bag. Combine the sugar and cinnamon. When cool, roll doughnuts in the sugar-cinnamon.

*Be sure it's milk free.

—*Ruth Chapin*

Maple-Cider Sauce

1 1/2 cups apple juice	1/4 cup brown sugar, firmly packed
2 teaspoons cornstarch	1/8 cup lemon juice
2/3 cup corn syrup	

In a small saucepan over medium-high heat, combine apple juice and cornstarch, stirring until smooth. Add corn syrup, brown sugar, and lemon juice. Stir, and bring to a boil. Boil 1 minute.

Moist Apricot Bread

◆M◆◆E◆◆W◆◆P◆◆S◆◆N◆

1/2 cup milk-free, soy-free
   margarine
1 cup sugar
2 cups barley flour
1 teaspoon baking soda
1/2 teaspoon salt

2 teaspoons baking powder
1/4 cup water
2 teaspoons vanilla extract
1 cup canned apricots, puréed
1/4 cup water

Preheat oven to 350°. Grease a 9x5x3-inch loaf pan. Cream margarine and sugar; set aside. In a separate bowl sift together flour, baking soda, and salt; set aside. Dissolve baking powder in water. Add vanilla extract and combine with sugar and margarine mixture. Add dry mixture; stir completely. Add apricots and remaining water; blend well. Pour into pan and bake 1 hour or until cake tester inserted in center comes out clean.

Pumpkin Bread

◆M◆◆E◆◆W◆◆P◆◆S◆◆N◆

1/2 cup milk-free, soy-free
   margarine
1 cup sugar
1/2 teaspoon cinnamon
1/2 teaspoon nutmeg
1/4 teaspoon ginger
1 3/4 cups barley flour

1 teaspoon baking soda
1/2 teaspoon salt
2 teaspoons baking powder
1/2 cup water
1 teaspoon vanilla extract
1 cup canned pumpkin

Preheat oven to 350°. Cream margarine and add sugar. Set aside. Sift together cinnamon, nutmeg, ginger, flour, baking soda, and salt; set aside. Dissolve baking powder in 1/4 cup water; add to margarine mixture. Mix remaining 1/4 cup water and vanilla extract together; add pumpkin. Stir well. Add to margarine mixture. Combine dry ingredients and wet ingredients. Blend together well. Pour into a loaf pan. Bake 1 hour.

Barley-Zucchini Bread

◆M◆E◆W◆P◆S◆N◆

3 cups barley flour
1/2 teaspoon baking powder
1 teaspoon salt
2 teaspoons cinnamon
1 teaspoon baking soda
2 cups peeled, grated zucchini
  (about 3 medium)

4 1/2 tablespoons water, 4 1/2 tablespoons oil, 1 tablespoon baking
  powder; mixed together
1 cup oil
1 tablespoon vanilla extract
2 cups sugar

Preheat oven to 350°. Sift together flour, baking powder, salt, cinnamon, and baking soda. Add zucchini; water, oil, and baking powder mixture; oil; vanilla extract; and sugar. Mix well. Pour into three loaf pans. Bake 65 minutes or until a cake tester inserted into center comes out clean. Makes 3 loaves.

Suggestion: Add 1/4 teaspoon unsweetened cocoa powder to make chocolate zucchini bread.

Tea Loaf

◆M◆E◆P◆S◆N◆

1/2 cup shortening
1 cup sugar
3 tablespoons water, 3 tablespoons oil,
  2 teaspoons baking powder;
  mixed together

1 1/2 cups flour
1 1/2 teaspoons baking powder
1/4 teaspoon salt
1/2 cup water
1/4 teaspoon grated lemon peel

Preheat oven to 350°. Grease a 9x5x3-inch loaf pan. Beat shortening until fluffy; gradually add sugar, beating well. Add water, oil, and baking powder mixture and mix well. Set aside. Combine flour, baking powder, and salt; add to creamed mixture. Stir in water and lemon peel.

Pour batter into loaf pan. Bake 55 minutes or until a cake tester inserted in center comes out clean. Cool in pan on a wire rack; remove and cool completely on wire rack. Top with Lemon Glaze, if desired (page 50).

Lemon Glaze

◆M◆E◆W◆P◆S◆N◆

1 cup sifted confectioners sugar   1 tablespoon lemon juice

Combine the ingredients. Stir until smooth. Add more sugar if desired.

Cranberry Muffins

◆M◆E◆P◆S◆N◆

1 1/2 tablespoons water, 1 1/2 table-   1/2 cup sugar
  spoons oil, 1 teaspoon baking   2 teaspoons baking powder
  powder; mixed together   1/2 teaspoon salt
1/2 cup orange juice   1/2 teaspoon grated orange peel
1/4 cup oil   1 cup canned whole cranberry
1 1/2 cups flour   sauce

Preheat oven to 400°. Line muffin tin with paper liners. Combine water, oil, and baking powder mixture with orange juice and oil. Mix in remaining ingredients. Stir just until flour is moistened. Batter should be lumpy. Fill muffin cups 2/3 full. Bake 20 to 25 minutes or until golden brown. Remove immediately from pan.

Note: These muffins can be frozen.

Apple Streusel Muffins

◆M◆E◆P◆S◆N◆

1 1/2 cups flour   3 tablespoons water, 3 tablespoons
1/2 cup sugar   oil, 2 teaspoons baking powder;
2 teaspoons baking powder   mixed together
1 teaspoon ground cinnamon   1/4 cup milk-free, soy-free
1/4 teaspoon ground allspice   margarine, melted
1/4 teaspoon baking soda   1 cup diced unpeeled apple
1/4 teaspoon salt   Streusel Topping (page 51)
1 cup water

Preheat oven to 375°. Line muffin tin with paper liners. Mix flour, sugar, baking powder, cinnamon, allspice, baking soda, and salt in a large bowl. Set aside. In another bowl, combine wet ingredients and whisk until well blended. Stir in diced apple. Pour wet mix over flour mixture and stir until dry ingredients are moistened. Pour the batter into muffin cups.

Streusel Topping

1/4 cup flour

3 tablespoons sugar

1/4 teaspoon ground cinnamon

2 tablespoons milk-free, soy-free margarine at room temperature

Put streusel topping ingredients into a medium-size bowl. Mix with a fork, then crumble with your fingers until mixture is the size of peas. Top each muffin with about 2 teaspoons of the streusel topping. Bake 20 to 25 minutes, or until browned. Remove from pans and let cool at least 1 hour before serving. Makes 18 muffins.

Note: These muffins can be frozen.

Banana Rice Bread

Ⓜ Ⓔ Ⓦ Ⓟ Ⓢ Ⓝ

4 bananas

1 cup brown sugar

1 cup shortening

1/2 cup oil

1 1/2 cups water

1 tablespoon vanilla extract

1 teaspoon ground cloves

2 tablespoons cinnamon

4 cups rice flour

2 tablespoons baking powder

Preheat oven to 350°. Grease a 9x13-inch pan. Mash bananas well and cream together with brown sugar, shortening, oil, water, vanilla extract, and spices. Sift together flour and baking powder. Stir flour mixture into banana mixture, mixing well. The batter should be a soft dough consistency. Spread into greased pan. Bake 45 minutes.

Peachy Muffins

◆M◆E◆P◆S◆N◆

1/3 cup milk-free, soy-free
   margarine
1/2 cup sugar
1 1/2 tablespoons water, 1 1/2 tablespoons oil,1 teaspoon baking
   powder; mixed together
1 1/2 cups flour

1 1/2 teaspoons baking powder
1/2 teaspoon salt
1/4 teaspoon ground nutmeg
1/2 cup water
1/2 cup canned peaches,
   chopped
Topping (recipe below)

Preheat oven to 350°. Line muffin tin with paper liners. Cream margarine and sugar. Add water, oil, and baking powder mixture; blend well. Set aside. Combine flour, baking powder, salt, and nutmeg; stir flour mixture into margarine mixture. Blend well. Stir in water and peaches. Fill muffin cups 2/3 full. Bake 25 minutes. Let cool before adding topping.

Topping

◆M◆E◆W◆P◆S◆N◆

1/2 cup sugar
1 teaspoon ground cinnamon

1/2 cup margarine

Mix sugar with cinnamon. Set aside. Melt margarine. Dip tops of muffins into melted margarine, then dip muffins into topping mixture.

Jelly-Filled Muffins

1/2 cup shortening
1 cup sugar
1 teaspoon vanilla extract
2 teaspoons baking powder
1/4 teaspoon salt
2 cups rice flour

1/2 cup water
3 tablespoons water, 1 tablespoon
    oil, 1 1/2 teaspoons baking
    powder; mixed together
about 4 tablespoons grape, raspberry,
    or strawberry jelly

Preheat oven to 375°. Line a muffin tin with paper liners. Beat the shortening and sugar until fluffy. Add all remaining ingredients except jelly. Spoon the batter into the muffin cups until 1/3 full. Drop about 1 teaspoon of your favorite jelly into the center of the muffin cups and top with remaining batter. Bake 30 minutes.

Corn Cakes

2 1/2 cups stone ground cornmeal
1 teaspoon salt
1 1/4 cups boiling water

1/4 cup oil
3/4 cup cold water

Preheat oven to 400°. Grease two cookie sheets. Mix cornmeal and salt; add boiling water. Combine oil and cold water and add to mixture. Form batter into 3-inch round flat cakes. Bake 25 minutes or until edges are brown. Serve hot for breakfast with preserves.

George Washington's Cherry Coffee Cake

◆M◆◆E◆◆P◆◆S◆◆N◆

1 1/4 cups flour
1/2 cup sugar
1 teaspoon baking powder
1/4 teaspoon baking soda
1/4 teaspoon salt
1/2 cup water

1/2 cup milk-free, soy-free
    margarine, melted
1 1/2 tablespoons water, 1 1/2 table-
    spoons oil, 1 teaspoon baking
    powder; mixed together
1 teaspoon vanilla extract

Preheat oven to 350°. Grease and flour 9x9-inch baking pan. In large bowl, mix flour with sugar, baking powder, baking soda, and salt. Add water; margarine; water, oil, and baking powder mixture; and vanilla extract. Beat until well mixed. Pour batter evenly into the baking pan.

Topping

1/2 cup flour
1/2 cup sugar
2 tablespoons milk-free, soy-free
    margarine, softened

1/4 teaspoon lemon extract
21- or 22-ounce can cherry pie
    filling

In a small bowl, mash flour, sugar, and margarine with a fork until mixture resembles coarse crumbs. Sprinkle half the mixture on top of the batter in baking pan. Stir the lemon extract into cherry pie filling; spread it over the batter. Top with the rest of flour mixture. Bake 1 hour or until top is light golden. Let cake cool completely before serving.

Rye Bread Sticks

Ⓜ Ⓔ Ⓦ Ⓟ Ⓢ Ⓝ

1 tablespoon yeast	1 tablespoon sugar
1/2 cup plus 2 tablespoons warm water	1 teaspoon salt
	1 1/2 cups rye flour

Preheat oven to 425°. Lightly grease cookie sheet. Combine all ingredients to make dough. If needed, add more water or flour to make dough manageable. Break off pieces of dough and roll into bread sticks. Place on cookie sheets and bake 10 minutes.

Suggestion: Brush bread sticks with water and roll them in sesame seeds before baking.

Main Meals

◆◆◆

Make sweet-potato chips by cutting sweet potatoes into thin slices and baking them in a hot oven.

Keep meals simple. Broil or grill meats; avoid dishes requiring cream sauces.

Use crumbled potato chips, crushed Rice Krispies, or crushed cornflakes as a coating for chicken.

Treat sweet potatoes as regular potatoes. Bake them and add margarine.

Spaghetti squash with tomato sauce is a good substitute for wheat pasta.

Tuna Rolls

◆M◆ E ◆P◆ N

6-ounce can tuna fish* packed in water
Italian salad dressing

2 slices milk-free, egg-free bread

Drain the tuna well. Add enough Italian salad dressing to the tuna to make it moist. Cut the crust off the bread. Spread the tuna mixture thinly onto the bread. Roll the bread as you would a jelly roll. Pinch the ends to secure in place and slice into thin wheels.

*Note: Read labels carefully, some tuna contains milk or soy.

Pineapple Sweet Potato Casserole

◆M◆ E ◆W◆ ◆P◆ ◆S◆ N

2 pounds (about 3 large) sweet potatoes
2 tablespoons milk-free, soy-free
   margarine, melted
1/4 cup sugar
1 1/2 teaspoons salt (or to taste)
10-ounce can crushed pineapple,
   drained

1/4 teaspoon cinnamon
1/4 teaspoon nutmeg
1/4 teaspoon mace
2 tablespoons milk-free,
   soy-free margarine, melted
2 tablespoons sugar

Peel and boil sweet potatoes until tender. Preheat oven to 375°. Grease an 11x7-inch pan. Whip together potatoes, 2 tablespoons margarine, 1/4 cup sugar, and salt. Add pineapple and spices. Turn mixture into greased pan. Combine the remaining margarine and sugar. Sprinkle over the top and bake 30 minutes. Serves 6.

Note: This can be frozen or refrigerated. Prior to baking, return to room temperature and bake at least 30 minutes or until heated through.

—Janice Berger

Turkey Soup

◆M◆E◆W◆P◆S◆N◆

1 1/2 pounds ground turkey
4 ribs celery, sliced
1 tablespoon olive oil
4 cups water
4 carrots, sliced
1/4 cup uncooked rice
1 small bay leaf
1/2 teaspoon thyme
1/2 teaspoon sweet basil
4 teaspoons chili powder

1/4 teaspoon onion powder
1/4 teaspoon dillweed
4 drops red pepper sauce
2 medium potatoes, diced
1 teaspoon salt (or to taste)
1/4 teaspoon pepper
3 1/2 cups tomatoes or tomato juice
1 can green beans
1 can black-eyed peas (or other beans)

Brown turkey and celery in 1 tablespoon olive oil. Add water, carrots, rice, bay leaf, thyme, basil, chili powder, onion powder, dillweed, red pepper sauce, potatoes, salt, and pepper. Bring to a boil and simmer until vegetables are tender. Add remaining ingredients and heat through. Remove bay leaf and serve hot.

Note: Chicken may be substituted for turkey.

—Kathie Brough

Cream Sauce

◆M◆E◆W◆P◆S◆N◆

3 tablespoons milk-free, soy-free margarine

1/4 cup rice flour
1 cup chicken broth

In a small saucepan, cook margarine and rice flour until thick over low heat. (It will take at least 10 minutes for this to become thick.) Add chicken broth to the flour mixture. Cook until thick and smooth.

Cream of Mushroom Soup

◆Ⓜ◆Ⓔ◆Ⓦ◆Ⓟ◆Ⓝ◆

1/4 cup minced onion

1/2 teaspoon celery seed

1/8 teaspoon garlic salt

3 tablespoons milk-free margarine

4 ounces chopped mushrooms

2 tablespoons rice flour

1 cup chicken broth

3/4 teaspoon salt

1 1/2 cups nondairy creamer

In a medium saucepan, sauté onion, celery, and garlic salt in margarine until soft. Add mushrooms and brown. Blend in flour, stirring continuously over low heat until mixed. Add broth, salt, and nondairy creamer. Slowly bring to a boil and simmer 2 minutes, stirring continuously.

Makes 2 1/2 cups, which is equal to 2 cans of mushroom soup.

Note: Rice flour can be replaced with barley or wheat flour.

—Robin Chadwell

Lasagna

◆Ⓜ◆Ⓔ◆Ⓟ◆Ⓝ◆

3 pounds firm tofu

1/4 cup lemon juice

4 teaspoons honey

6 tablespoons oil

4 teaspoons basil

1 teaspoon garlic powder

1/2 teaspoon nutmeg

2 teaspoons salt

1 pound milk-free, egg-free
   lasagna noodles

3 cups spaghetti sauce

Cook lasagna noodles according to package directions; drain and set aside. Preheat oven to 350°. Lightly grease a 9x13-inch pan.

Process tofu in a food processor until smooth. Pour into a mixing bowl and add lemon juice, honey, oil, basil, garlic powder, nutmeg, and salt. Stir until well mixed; set aside.

Layer as follows in the pan: spaghetti sauce, lasagna noodles, tofu mixture. Repeat layers, ending with spaghetti sauce.

Bake for 35 minutes. Remove from oven; allow to set before serving.

◆ Milk-Free ◆ Egg-Free ◆ Wheat-Free

Chicken and Rice

◆M◆◆E◆◆W◆◆P◆◆S◆◆N◆

1 teaspoon oregano

2 peppercorns

1 clove garlic, peeled

2 teaspoons salt

2 teaspoons olive oil

1 teaspoon vinegar

2 1/2 pounds chicken, cut into serving
   pieces

1 tablespoon olive oil

2 ounces cured ham, diced

1 strip bacon, diced

1 onion, peeled

1 green pepper, seeded

1 celery stalk

1 cup water

6-ounce can tomato paste

6 green olives

1 teaspoon capers

1 tomato, chopped

2 tablespoons olive oil

2 1/4 cups rice

1 can pinto beans, kidney beans,
   or green peas, drained

3 cups water

Mash together the oregano, peppercorns, garlic, salt, 2 tea-spoons olive oil, and vinegar.

Rub chicken with mashed ingredients. Place 1 tablespoon olive oil in a large deep kettle. Add diced ham and bacon and brown over high heat. Add chicken and brown lightly. Reduce heat to moderate.

In blender, grind onion, pepper, celery, 1 cup water, and tomato paste. Add onion mixture to kettle. Add olives, capers, and chopped tomato, and cook for 10 minutes. Add 2 tablespoons olive oil, rice, and beans. Cook for 5 minutes.

Heat water to boiling and add to kettle. (Water level should just cover ingredients.) Mix well and cook rapidly, uncovered, until food begins to boil. With a large spoon, turn rice from bottom to top. Cover and cook slowly for 20 minutes.

Turn rice once more, cover, and cook for 10 minutes longer or until rice is cooked. Serve at once.

Note: 1 chopped and seeded sweet chili pepper may be added when adding onion and green pepper.

Greg's Nacho Casserole

◆M◆◆E◆◆W◆◆P◆◆S◆◆N◆

1 wedge lettuce
1 pint cherry tomatoes
1 pound ground beef
16-ounce can kidney beans

1 teaspoon chili powder
1/2 teaspoon salt
1/2 teaspoon garlic powder
corn chips

Preheat oven to 425°. Rinse and dry lettuce and tomatoes. Tear lettuce into small pieces. Quarter tomatoes. Set the vegetables aside.

Brown ground beef in skillet and drain grease. Add drained kidney beans to meat. Add chili powder, salt, and garlic powder. Spread a layer of corn chips in a casserole dish. Put the cooked meat on top of the chips. Heat in the oven for 4 to 5 minutes. Layer lettuce and tomatoes on top of casserole.

Note: An allowed salad dressing or taco sauce may be added for more flavor. Add onions, peppers, or any other toppings to suit your taste.

—Greg Scherrer

Fried Potatoes

◆M◆◆E◆◆W◆◆P◆◆S◆◆N◆

5 medium potatoes
2 tablespoons milk-free, soy-free
   margarine
2 tablespoons vegetable oil

1/8 teaspoon paprika
salt and coarsely ground pepper
   to taste

Scrub potatoes well. Cook whole potatoes, in their skins, in boiling salted water until cooked (15 to 20 minutes). Drain and cool. Slice potatoes about 1/8-inch thick (leave skin on).

In a large frying pan over medium heat, combine margarine, oil, and paprika. Add potatoes. Sprinkle lightly with salt and pepper.

Cook until they are brown and crusty on both sides (20 to 25 minutes). Turn carefully to keep slices from breaking.

Serves 4.

Spaghetti Sauce

◆M◆E◆W◆P◆S◆N◆

29-ounce can tomato purée
2 6-ounce cans tomato paste
water
2 tablespoons sugar

salt and pepper to taste
2 teaspoons each of basil, minced
    fresh garlic, oregano, minced
    fresh onion, and parsley

In a large pot, mix tomato paste and tomato purée. Fill each can with water and add to pot. Add remaining ingredients. Bring to a boil, reduce heat to low, and cover. Let sauce simmer slowly for 4 hours, stirring occasionally.

Note: Look in health food stores for pastas that are free of your allergen (e.g., wheat-free, egg-free).

Baked Potato Skins

◆M◆E◆W◆P◆S◆N◆

6 small baking potatoes
1/4 cup milk-free, soy-free margarine

1/4 teaspoon paprika
1/8 teaspoon white pepper

Preheat oven to 400°. Scrub potatoes and rub lightly with a little of the margarine. Pierce the potatoes in several places with a fork.

Bake potatoes for 45 to 60 minutes or until tender when pierced. When cool, cut in halves lengthwise and scoop out potato, leaving a thin shell about 1/8-inch thick.

Place potato skins on a baking sheet. Melt margarine in a small pan with paprika and white pepper. Brush insides of potato skins with margarine mixture.

Bake until crisp and golden (18 to 20 minutes).

Serves 6.

Suggestion: For variety, add crumbled bacon, green onion, or chives.

Vegetable Soup

◆M◆E◆W◆P◆S◆N◆

16-ounce can tomatoes

1-2 pounds beef shanks, short ribs or
meaty bones

2 carrots, sliced

3 stalks celery with tops, sliced

2 medium onions, diced

2 medium potatoes, diced

3 cups water (more may be added)

1 teaspoon salt

1/2 teaspoon pepper

10-ounce package frozen mixed
vegetables*

Liquefy canned tomatoes with liquid in blender. Add tomatoes with all remaining ingredients to large kettle or Crockpot. Cover, bring to a boil, and simmer over low heat 3 to 4 hours on stove or in Crockpot on low for 12 to 24 hours. Longer simmering allows flavors to develop. Stir occasionally and add more water as needed. Remove meat from bones and return meat to soup. Add salt and pepper to taste.

*Instead of the frozen mixed vegetables, use any vegetables you have on hand. Use any combination of corn, lima beans, green beans, zucchini, or other available vegetables. Add water or tomato purée to adjust liquid to the desired amount.

—*Debbie Scherrer*

Parsley-Potato Stuffing

◆M◆E◆W◆P◆S◆N◆

6 medium potatoes

2/3 cup finely chopped onion

6 tablespoons finely chopped fresh
parsley

1/4 cup milk-free, soy-free margarine

salt

pepper

Peel the potatoes. Boil the potatoes in salted water. Drain; dice the potatoes, and set aside. In a large frying pan, gently fry the onion and parsley in margarine. Add potatoes; stir to coat the potatoes evenly. Season to taste. Place potato stuffing in poultry, and roast.

◆M◆ Milk-Free ◆E◆ Egg-Free ◆W◆ Wheat-Free

Tuna Soup

◆Ⓜ Ⓔ Ⓦ Ⓟ Ⓢ Ⓝ◆

2 tablespoons oil
1/2 small onion, minced
1 celery stalk, minced
1 garlic clove, minced
10 1/2-ounce can condensed chicken
   broth, undiluted*
1 soup can of tomato juice

1/2 teaspoon dried basil
1 teaspoon salt
10-ounce package frozen mixed
   vegetables
2 6 1/2- or 7-ounce cans water-
   packed tuna, drained

In a saucepan, heat oil. Add onion, celery, and garlic; cook until soft. Add chicken broth and remaining ingredients; bring to a boil. Reduce heat; simmer, covered, for 10 minutes. Makes 6 servings.

Note: You may want to decrease the amount of spices for young children. One-quarter teaspoon thyme and/or 1/4 teaspoon pepper may be added.

*Read the label to be sure it's wheat-free.

Turkey Tots

◆Ⓜ Ⓔ Ⓦ Ⓟ Ⓢ Ⓝ◆

1 pound ground turkey
1/4 cup quick oats
lemon pepper
black pepper

salt
1/2 cup barley flour
oil

Combine turkey and oats. Season to taste. Form turkey into small balls. Roll in barley flour and coat well. Flatten and coat in flour again. Heat 1 inch of oil in skillet or deep fryer; drop turkey tots into hot oil. Turn to brown evenly.

—Carol Fite

Poppyseed Muffins

◆M◆E◆P◆S◆N◆

1 1/2 cups flour
1/3 cup poppy seeds
1/3 cup sugar
1 tablespoon baking powder
1/2 teaspoon salt
1 cup water

1 1/2 tablespoons water, 1 1/2 table-
    spoons oil, 1 teaspoon baking
    powder; mixed together
1/4 cup milk-free, soy-free margarine,
    melted

Preheat oven to 400°. Line muffin tin with paper liners. Stir together flour, poppy seeds, sugar, baking powder, and salt. Set aside. Mix together water; water, oil, and baking powder mixture; and margarine. Add to dry mixture. Fill muffin cups 2/3 full. Bake 15 to 18 minutes or until a cake tester inserted in center comes out clean.

Suggestion: This recipe also works well as a breakfast treat.

Sweet Potato Muffins

◆M◆E◆P◆S◆N◆

1 cup flour, sifted
1 teaspoon baking powder
1/4 teaspoon baking soda
1/2 teaspoon salt
1/2 teaspoon ground cinnamon
1/2 teaspoon ground nutmeg, optional
1/4 cup sugar
1/4 cup water

1/2 cup cooked mashed sweet
    potatoes (about 1 large potato)
1 1/2 tablespoons water, 1 1/2 table-
    spoons oil, 1 teaspoon baking
    powder; mixed together
2 tablespoons milk-free, soy-free
    margarine, melted

Preheat oven to 350°. Line muffin tin with paper liners. In medium bowl, sift together flour, baking powder, baking soda, salt, cinnamon, and nutmeg. Set aside. Combine sugar with all remaining ingredients in another bowl. Add to flour mixture; stir until well moistened. Fill muffin tins 2/3 full. Bake 25 minutes.

Hush Puppies

2 cups cornmeal
1 teaspoon salt
1 tablespoon shortening

2 cups boiling water
1 cup oil

Mix together cornmeal, salt, and shortening; add boiling water. Press into small oval shapes. In a large kettle, heat oil until it sizzles. Drop hush puppies into oil and cook until golden brown. Drain on paper towels. Serve warm.

Suggestion: These are great for snacks. They can also be served with lunch or dinner. For a spicy flavor, add 1 teaspoon minced onion and 4 drops hot sauce.

Caribbean Fritters

oil for frying
1 cup cornmeal
1/2 cup flour
1 teaspoon baking powder

1 cup water
salt to taste
1/2 cup chopped broccoli

In a deep pot, heat 1 to 1 1/2 inches of cooking oil. In a medium bowl, combine other ingredients except broccoli. Stir well. Add broccoli and stir until well covered in batter. Scoop mixture by spoonfuls into hot oil. Fry until golden brown, turning once.

Notes: For wheat-free fritters, substitute flour with cornmeal; adjust water if necessary. Chopped spinach leaves may be substituted for broccoli.

—Terry Hess

Wheat-Free Pizza Dough

◆M◆ ◆E◆ ◆W◆ ◆P◆ ◆S◆ ◆N◆

2 cups quick oats
1 teaspoon sugar

1/4 teaspoon salt
1 cup boiling water

Preheat oven to 400°. Grease a 12-inch pizza pan. Grind oats 20 seconds in food processor. Put oats, sugar, and salt into bowl. Add boiling water and mix vigorously. Form into a ball, and let cool for 1 minute. Press down onto pizza pan and roll out to cover bottom of pan. A small pizza pastry roller works well for this. Prick the crust with a fork. Bake 5 minutes. Add allowed toppings.

—*Kristine Determan*

Deep-Dish Pizza Dough

◆M◆ ◆E◆ ◆P◆ ◆S◆ ◆N◆

1 package dry yeast
1 cup warm water
1/4 cup vegetable oil

2 tablespoons olive oil
1/4 cup cornmeal
2 3/4 cups flour, divided

In a large mixing bowl, dissolve yeast in water. Add oils, cornmeal, and 1 3/4 cups flour to mixing bowl. Beat 10 minutes. Add remaining flour; knead 10 to 15 minutes. (If dough is sticky, add a few tablespoons flour.) Let rise in a warm place until doubled. Punch down and let rise again.

Preheat oven to 475°. Grease two 10-inch cake pans. Divide dough in half; place half in center of each pan, and roll to 1/8-inch thickness. Push dough up onto sides of pans. Top with Carol's Cheese-Free Pizza Topping (next page) or other allowed toppings. Bake 20 to 40 minutes, depending on the toppings.

—*Celide Barnes Koerner*

Carol's Cheese-Free Pizza Topping

⬧M⬧ ⬧E⬧ ⬧W⬧ ⬧P⬧ ⬧S⬧ ⬧N⬧

1/2 pound lean ground beef	1 cup tomato or pizza sauce
sliced vegetables (mushrooms,	basil
peppers, zucchini, etc.)	oregano
olive oil	

Preheat oven to 475°. While pizza crust dough is rising (see Deep-Dish Pizza Dough, page 68), brown beef and set aside. Sauté vegetables in a little oil until tender. When dough is ready, spread tomato or pizza sauce on top. Sprinkle with basil and oregano. Top with meat and vegetables. Brush top of pizza lightly with olive oil. Bake 20 minutes or until done.

Notes: Vegetables and beef can be prepared in microwave. Pizza slices can be individually wrapped and frozen for later use.

—Virginia Haas

Gnocchi di Patate

⬧M⬧ ⬧E⬧ ⬧P⬧ ⬧S⬧ ⬧N⬧

2 pounds large Idaho potatoes,	2 teaspoons salt, divided
unpeeled	1 1/2 cups flour

Put the potatoes into a pot with enough cold water to cover and add 1 teaspoon salt. Bring to a boil over medium heat and cook until tender. Drain, allow to cool slightly, and remove skin. Mash potatoes or put through ricer onto a floured pasta board or marble surface. While still warm, work the flour in until dough ball becomes firm.

Divide the dough into eight pieces and roll between well-floured hands to form long cylinders about a half-inch in diameter. Cut these into one-inch-long pieces. Sprinkle liberally with flour. Add remaining salt to a fresh pot of water and bring to a boil. Drop the gnocchi into rapidly boiling water and remove with slotted spoon 30 seconds after they float to surface. Drain and toss with allowed spaghetti sauce or sauce of your choice.

—Terry Hess

Carol's Spicy Barbecue Sauce

M E W P S N

1 cup tomato sauce
1/2 cup plus 2 tablespoons honey
1/2 teaspoon chili powder
1/2 teaspoon paprika

1 1/2 teaspoons vegetable oil
1/8 teaspoon garlic powder
1 tablespoon minced onion

Mix all ingredients together in a bowl; cover and refrigerate until ready to use.

—*Virginia* Haas

Potato Puffs

M E W P S N

1 pound potatoes, peeled, quartered
    and cooked in unsalted water
1 tablespoon milk-free, soy-free
    margarine
1/8 teaspoon pepper
1/2 teaspoon sugar

1 teaspoon salt
1 1/2 tablespoons water mixed
    with 1 tablespoon oil
2 tablespoons cornstarch
1/2 cup cornstarch
2 cups oil

Drain and coarsely mash potatoes. Add margarine, pepper, sugar, salt, water and oil mixture, and 2 tablespoons cornstarch. Mix and let stand until cool.

Form potato mixture into 1-inch balls and roll in remaining cornstarch. Heat oil in a large kettle to 375° or until a drop of batter sizzles. Fry potato puffs until golden brown. Drain on paper towels and serve warm.

Cold Sesame Noodles

ⓂⒺⓌⓅⓈⓃ

1/2 pound rice noodles
3 tablespoons scallions, minced
1 carrot, grated
1 clove garlic, minced
2 tablespoons minced fresh ginger root
1/4 cup water

2 tablespoons Sesame-Sunflower
 Tahini (recipe below)
2 tablespoons safflower oil
2 tablespoons rice or cider vinegar
1 tablespoon sugar

In a large pot, soak rice noodles in cold water for at least 15 minutes. Boil until tender, about 10 to 15 minutes. Drain and rinse with cool water. Transfer noodles to medium-size mixing bowl. Add scallions and carrot. Toss well. Set aside. In a small bowl, mix the remaining ingredients to make a dressing. Pour over the noodles and toss until well coated. Chill for 1 hour before serving.

—Jennifer Borgesen

Sesame-Sunflower Tahini

ⓂⒺⓅⓈⓃ

1/4 cup unhulled sesame seeds
1/4 cup sunflower seeds
2 tablespoons safflower or canola oil

2 tablespoons honey
3 to 4 tablespoons water

Preheat oven to 300°. Pour seeds into an oven-proof pan. Bake until lightly browned. Stir every 5 minutes. Remove from oven and allow to cool.

Place toasted seeds in a blender or food processor with a metal blade. Grind seeds until they resemble a coarse meal. Add oil and honey; blend well. At this point it should resemble a paste. Add water, one tablespoon at a time, until the mixture becomes creamy. Transfer to an airtight container and store in the refrigerator to keep the mixture from separating. Makes 1/2 cup tahini.

Sweet Potato Biscuits

◆M◆E◆P◆S◆N◆

1 large sweet potato (about 1/2 pound), baked and peeled	1/2 teaspoon nutmeg
1 1/2 cups flour, sifted	1/4 teaspoon ginger
2 1/2 teaspoons baking powder	1/3 cup dark brown sugar, firmly packed
1/2 teaspoon salt	1/2 cup milk-free, soy-free margarine, softened and cut into pieces
1/2 teaspoon cinnamon	2 tablespoons orange juice

Mash sweet potato until smooth. Measure 3/4 cup sweet potato; set aside to cool. Preheat oven to 450°. Sift together flour, baking powder, salt, cinnamon, nutmeg, and ginger into a medium bowl. Stir in brown sugar. Cut in margarine until mixture resembles coarse meal. Add 3/4 cup sweet potato and orange juice; stir until evenly moistened.

Turn onto lightly floured surface and knead gently, just until dough holds together. Roll out dough to 1/2-inch thickness. Cut dough to form 2-inch biscuits. Place biscuits 1 inch apart on an ungreased baking sheet. Bake 8 to 10 minutes or until golden brown. Allow to cool before serving.

Note: These are great snacks to pack in a lunchbox or take on a trip.

—*Carol Stull*

Butternut Squash Loaf

◆M◆E◆P◆S◆N◆

1-2 pounds butternut squash	2 cups flour
1/2 cup milk-free, soy-free margarine, softened	1 teaspoon cinnamon
1 1/2 cups sugar	1/2 teaspoon nutmeg
3 tablespoons oil, 3 tablespoons water, 2 teaspoons baking powder; mixed together	1/2 teaspoon allspice
	1/4 teaspoon ground ginger

Preheat oven to 400°. Cut squash in half; remove seeds. Place cut side down in shallow baking pan, add 1/2 inch water, and cover with foil. Bake 1 hour or until tender. Drain, scoop out squash, and mash. Throw away shell. Measure 1 3/4 cups squash and set aside. Refrigerate any remaining squash for other uses.

Grease and flour 9x5x3-inch loaf pan. Set aside. Beat margarine and sugar until creamy. Add oil, water, and baking powder mixture; stir well. Add remaining ingredients, including 1 3/4 cups squash. Stir well. Spoon into loaf pan. Bake 1 hour or until cake tester inserted into center comes out clean. Cool on wire rack 10 minutes. Remove from pan and let cool completely.

David's Corn Bread

◆Ⓜ Ⓔ ◆Ⓟ Ⓢ ◆Ⓝ

2 tablespoons milk-free, soy-free
   margarine
3/4 cup cornmeal
1 1/2 cups flour
3/4 cup sugar
2 1/4 teaspoons baking powder

1/2 teaspoon salt
1 cup water
3 tablespoons water, 3 tablespoons
   oil, 2 teaspoons baking powder;
   mixed together

Preheat oven to 400°. Put margarine into a 9-inch square baking pan and set pan in the oven while you preheat it. In large mixing bowl, sift together cornmeal, flour, sugar, baking powder, and salt. Set aside. In small bowl, combine 1 cup water and the water, oil, and baking powder mixture. Add melted margarine. (Tilt baking pan from side to side to be sure bottom of pan is greased before pouring out remaining margarine.) Combine wet and dry ingredients. Stir well. Pour batter into baking pan. Bake 25 minutes.

—David Leavitt

Potato Stuffing

◆M◆E◆W◆P◆S◆N◆

8 medium potatoes
2 tablespoons milk-free, soy-free margarine
3/4 cup finely chopped celery
1/2 cup finely chopped onion
1 teaspoon dried thyme

1 teaspoon dried sage
1/4 teaspoon black pepper
1 teaspoon poultry seasoning
1/2 teaspoon salt

Peel potatoes and cook in boiling water until tender. Drain and let cool. Cut into small pieces or cubes. Set aside. In a large frying pan, melt margarine. Add celery and onions and cook gently until soft. Remove from heat. Add remaining seasonings. Stir well. Add potatoes; stir until well coated. Stuff turkey or chicken and cook immediately.

Turkey Seasoning

◆M◆E◆W◆P◆S◆N◆

1 small clove of garlic, peeled
1 small peppercorn
1/2 teaspoon oregano

1 teaspoon salt
1 teaspoon olive oil
1/2 teaspoon vinegar

Mix all ingredients together in small bowl. Mash with a mortar. Use a pastry brush or your hands to rub seasoning evenly over turkey. Stuff and cook turkey as usual.

Note: This seasoning gives the turkey a little more flavor and adds a golden brown color to the turkey skin.

Easy Vegetable Soup

◆M◆ ◆E◆ ◆P◆ ◆S◆ ◆N◆

15-ounce can kidney beans, undrained
2 1/2 cups water
1 1/2 cups diced zucchini
1 small onion, chopped
3/4 cup sliced celery
1/2 cup diced carrot

1 garlic clove, minced
8-ounce can tomato sauce
1 cup uncooked small milk-free, egg-
 free pasta noodles
2 teaspoons salt

Pour kidney beans and liquid into a blender and purée. Spoon purée into a large pot. Add water, zucchini, onion, celery, carrot, garlic, and tomato sauce. Bring to a fast boil. Reduce heat, cover, and simmer 20 minutes. Stir in pasta and salt. Cook, uncovered, until pasta is soft. Serve immediately.

Note: For a wheat-free soup, use a specialty rice- or corn-based pasta, or add cooked rice instead of pasta.

Northern-Style Corn Bread

◆M◆ ◆E◆ ◆W◆ ◆P◆ ◆S◆ ◆N◆

2 cups yellow cornmeal
1/3 cup sugar
1 tablespoon baking powder
1 teaspoon salt

1/2 teaspoon xanthan gum*
1 cup grated zucchini
1 cup water
1/4 cup vegetable oil

Preheat oven to 425°. Grease an 8-inch square baking pan. Set aside. Combine all the dry ingredients in a medium bowl. Set aside. In a separate bowl, combine zucchini, water, and oil. Pour wet ingredients into dry ingredients, stirring just until moistened. Pour batter into baking pan, spreading evenly. Bake 25 minutes or until golden.

*Xanthan gum may be purchased at a health food store or by calling Ener-G Foods.

—Shelley Meade

Pizza Bread

◆M◆E◆P◆S◆N◆

2 cups flour	3/4 cup water
1 tablespoon baking powder	1/4 cup oil
1/2 teaspoon salt	1 tablespoon sugar
1 1/2 teaspoons oregano	
1 1/2 tablespoons water, 1 1/2 table-	
spoons oil, 1 teaspoon baking	
powder; mixed together	

Preheat oven to 400°. Grease 9-inch square baking pan. Set aside.

In large bowl, stir together flour, baking powder, salt, and oregano. Set aside. In medium bowl, mix water, oil, and baking powder mixture with water, oil, and sugar. Add this mixture to dry ingredients. Stir until just blended. Spread dough into prepared pan.

Pizza Sauce

◆M◆E◆W◆P◆S◆N◆

6-ounce can tomato paste	1/4 teaspoon oregano
1/4 teaspoon basil	1/4 teaspoon garlic powder

Combine all ingredients for pizza sauce. Spread over dough. Bake 30 minutes or until done. Cut into squares and serve.

Note: You can enjoy as is or add your favorite topping before baking.

Pizza Topping

◆M◆E◆W◆P◆S◆N◆

2 cloves garlic	1/4 cup lemon juice
3/4 teaspoon salt	1/2 cup oil
2 tablespoons water	
2 1/2 cups (1 can) drained, cooked	
chickpeas, rinsed well	

Mash garlic with salt and water until it forms a paste. In a blender or food processor, purée the chickpeas with lemon juice and garlic paste until smooth. With the motor running, add the oil in a stream until combined. Let it stand, covered, 1 hour before spreading on pizza dough.

Note: This is also good on pasta or as a dip or salad dressing.

—Marianne Cane

Kathy's Barbecued Wings

Ⓜ Ⓔ Ⓦ Ⓟ Ⓢ Ⓝ

5 pounds chicken wings
1 large onion, minced
3 tablespoons cooking oil
2 cloves garlic, minced

2 cups tomato sauce
1 cup molasses
1/4 cup lemon juice
1 teaspoon salt

Preheat oven to 350°. Place wings in single layer on a baking sheet lined with foil. Bake 25 to 35 minutes, or until juices run clear. Set aside. In frying pan, sauté onion in oil until translucent, but not brown. Add garlic and sauté for 2 to 3 minutes. Stir in remaining ingredients and bring to a boil. Reduce heat and simmer 10 minutes. Place cooked chicken on a broiler rack; coat one side with barbecue sauce. Set oven to broil. Broil chicken 10 minutes. Turn and coat with remaining sauce. Broil an additional 10 minutes. Serve with raw celery and carrots.

Note: Leftovers may be frozen.

—Kathy Lundquist

Skillet Potatoes

ⓂⒺⓌⓅⓈⓃ

3 pounds small baking potatoes,
    peeled and thinly sliced, divided
1/2 cup milk-free, soy-free
    margarine, melted, divided

3/4 teaspoon salt, divided
3/4 teaspoon pepper, divided

Preheat oven to 350°. Heat a 10-inch cast-iron skillet in oven 8 minutes or until hot. Arrange a third of potato slices in skillet. Drizzle with a third of the margarine, and sprinkle with 1/4 teaspoon salt and 1/4 teaspoon pepper. Repeat layering process with remaining ingredients. Bake 1 hour. Increase oven temperature to 500° and bake 5 minutes or until potatoes are brown. Allow to cool slightly before serving.

Stove-Top Beef Noodle Casserole

ⓂⒺⓅⓈⓃ

1-pound box ziti pasta
1 pound ground beef*

1/4 cup diced onion
1/2 cup green peas, cooked

Prepare pasta according to directions on box. While pasta is boiling, sauté beef and onion in a medium sized frying pan, until cooked. Drain fat, and keep over low heat. Drain pasta and add to beef and onion. Add peas. Stir until well blended. Serve immediately.

*Ground turkey can be substituted for ground beef.

—*Marguerite Furlong*

James's Favorite Pizza Crust

ⓂⒺⓅⓈⓃ

1 cup warm water
1 teaspoon sugar
1 package yeast

1 teaspoon salt
2 tablespoons olive oil
3 cups flour

In a bowl, mix together water and sugar. Sprinkle with yeast. Allow to sit 10 minutes. Add salt, olive oil, and flour. Knead until very smooth. Divide dough in half. Roll each piece into a 12-inch circle. Place on lightly greased baking sheet and let rise 20 minutes. Flatten each and top with Middle Eastern Pizza Topping (recipe below) or other toppings. Bake as directed.

Note: This crust may be made in a bread machine by doubling the recipe. Set the machine for mixing and kneading only. If dough is ready before you are, punch it down and let it rise again.

—James McCarten

Middle Eastern Pizza Topping

M E W P S N

3/4 pound ground beef	1 clove garlic, minced
1 cup finely chopped onion	1/4 teaspoon cumin
1/4 cup finely chopped green pepper	1/4 teaspoon coriander
16-ounce can ground tomatoes	1/8 teaspoon allspice
1/4 cup minced parsley	pepper to taste

Preheat oven to 425°. In a skillet, cook beef until no longer pink. Drain fat. Add remaining ingredients and simmer, covered, about 20 minutes. Spread topping on pizza crust and bake 15 minutes.

Suggestion: Make an extra pizza. Cut into slices and freeze. Heat in a microwave oven. This recipe makes an easy treat to take to birthday parties or school.

—James McCarten

Broccoli Salad

◆M◆ ◆E◆ ◆W◆ ◆P◆ ◆S◆ ◆N◆

2 heads broccoli
1 bunch scallions
1/2 cup raisins

1/2 cup cooked, diced bacon
(about 4 strips)

Cut broccoli into bite-size pieces; steam on stovetop or in microwave until tender. Drain and set aside to cool. Mince scallions and mix with broccoli. Add raisins and bacon. Serve chilled.

Note: Sprinkle with your favorite salad dressing before serving for extra flavor.

Cold Pasta Salad

◆M◆ ◆E◆ ◆P◆ ◆S◆ ◆N◆

1-pound box colored spiral noodles,
    cooked
1 head broccoli
2 fresh tomatoes, diced
6 green olives, sliced

4 black olives, sliced
1 cucumber, peeled and diced
olive oil
salt to taste (optional)

Run cooked pasta under cold water; drain and set aside. Chop broccoli heads into small pieces; steam or cook in microwave until tender. Drain and run under cold water. In large bowl, combine broccoli, noodles, tomatoes, olives, and cucumber. Stir until well blended. Sprinkle with olive oil and stir again. Season with salt. Refrigerate for a few hours if time allows.

Note: You can substitute olive oil with your own salad dressing.

Fajitas

◆M◆E◆W◆P◆S◆N◆

4 boneless, skinless chicken breasts	1 cup diced tomato
corn or flour tortillas, cooked	1/2 cup guacamole
2 cups diced lettuce	

In frying pan or on a grill, cook chicken breast until well done. Remove from heat and allow to cool. Once cooled, cut into strips. In center of each tortilla, place some lettuce, tomato, guacamole, and chicken strips. Roll tortillas and serve immediately or secure with toothpicks and pack for school lunch.

Note: Chicken may be substituted with black beans. To do so, heat beans, place in blender, and purée.

Guacamole

◆M◆E◆W◆P◆S◆N◆

2 large ripe avocados, mashed	2 tablespoons lemon juice
2 medium tomatoes, finely chopped	1/2 teaspoon salt
1 medium onion, finely chopped	dash of pepper
1 clove garlic, finely chopped	

In blender, purée all ingredients. Cover and refrigerate for 1 hour before serving.

Potato Fans

◆M◆E◆W◆P◆S◆N◆

1 large baking potato	salt
cooking oil	

Preheat oven to 350°. Scrub potato until clean. Rub with cooking oil and sprinkle with salt. Cut the potato into thin slices, being careful not to cut all the way through. Drizzle oil into the slices. Place potato onto oven rack. Place baking pan on oven shelf below potato to catch dripping oil. Cook until potato is soft. You will see potato slices fan open when potato is cooked. Potato will be soft when pricked with a fork.

Potato Chips

◆M◆ ◆E◆ ◆W◆ ◆P◆ ◆S◆ ◆N◆

1 pound potatoes, unpeeled, scrubbed	1 1/2 teaspoons oil
	1/2 teaspoon salt

Lightly grease a microwave-safe plate. Using a cheese slicer, cut potatoes into thin slices. Place slices in a large bowl. Fill with cold water to cover; set aside to soak for 30 minutes. Drain and dry on paper towels. In a medium bowl, combine potatoes, oil, and salt. Toss to coat evenly. Arrange slices on prepared plate in a single layer. Microwave on high 3 minutes. Flip slices and cook 1 minute or until crisp. Transfer to serving plate and cool. Repeat with remaining slices.

Suggestion: For variety, try using sweet potatoes.

Moist Rice Stuffing

◆M◆ ◆E◆ ◆W◆ ◆P◆ ◆S◆ ◆N◆

6 tablespoons milk-free, soy-free margarine	2 cups cold cooked rice
2 cups diced celery	2 teaspoons salt
1 cup diced onions	1/2 teaspoon pepper
1/4 pound ground beef or ground turkey	1/2 teaspoon marjoram
	1/4 teaspoon thyme leaves

In a medium saucepan, melt margarine. Sauté celery and onions until tender, stirring frequently. Add meat and cook until brown. Add remaining ingredients; stir until well blended. Makes enough stuffing for a 5-pound bird.

Wheat-Free Coating

◆M◆E◆W◆P◆S◆N◆

3/4 cup crunchy rice cereal or
    cornflakes
1/2 teaspoon white pepper

1/2 teaspoon paprika
1/4 teaspoon salt

Crush cereal finely; add remaining ingredients. Mix well. Use in meatballs, as a topping for casseroles, or as breading for fried chicken.

Cookies
and Snacks

❖❖❖

Make a hobby of buying unusual cookie cutters. Your child will be remembered for the fun-shaped cookies.

Keep plenty of cookie supplies on hand: sprinkles, powdered cocoa, confectioners sugar, and food coloring.

Make layered cookies by using nested cookie cutters: Reserve the biggest cookie for the bottom. Use a medium-size cookie for the top. Before baking, use the smallest cookie cutter and cut out the middle section of the top cookies. When baked, spread jelly, icing, or frosting on the largest cookie, and put the medium-size cookie on top. You will see the filling through the middle of the cookie. For special treats, dip the top cookie in chocolate frosting, and use white filling to make a black and white cookie.

Cinnamon Crunch Cookies

◆M◆E◆P◆S◆N◆

1 1/3 cups flour
1 teaspoon cream of tartar
1/2 teaspoon baking soda
1/8 teaspoon salt
1/2 cup milk-free, soy-free
   margarine, softened
3/4 cup sugar

1/2 teaspoon vanilla extract
1 1/2 tablespoons water, 1 1/2 tablespoons oil, 1 teaspoon baking
   powder; mixed together
2 teaspoons ground cinnamon
   mixed with 1/4 cup sugar

Preheat oven to 400°. Grease cookie sheets. Stir together flour, cream of tartar, baking soda, and salt; set aside. In mixer bowl, combine margarine and sugar; beat until fluffy. Blend in vanilla. Beat in water, oil, and baking powder mixture. Gradually add to flour mixture, beating until just combined.

Drop by rounded teaspoons into the cinnamon-sugar mixture. Roll cookies to coat well, shaping them into balls as you roll. Arrange balls about 1 1/2 inches apart on greased baking sheets. Bake 8 to 10 minutes or until edges are golden brown. Transfer to wire racks to cool. Makes about 3 dozen cookies.

Note: This cookie mixture can go from freezer to oven.

Easy Oatmeal Cookies

◆M◆E◆W◆P◆S◆N◆

4 cups oat flour*
1 1/4 cups sugar
1 teaspoon baking soda

1 cup oil
1 1/3 cups apple juice
1/4 cup quick oats

Combine all the ingredients except quick oats and mix with electric mixer. Let stand for 1 to 1 1/2 hours. Add 1/4 cup quick oats to the dough, and mix well.

Preheat oven to 350°. Place rounded spoonfuls of dough on a nonstick baking sheet. Cook for 10 minutes or until brown. Cool completely before removing from cookie sheet.

Suggestion: Add cocoa, raisins, or coconut flakes for variety.

*Oat flour can be made by finely grinding regular oats in a food processor.

Oatmeal Cookies

◆M◆◆E◆◆P◆◆S◆◆N◆

1/2 cup packed brown sugar

1/2 cup granulated sugar

1/2 cup milk-free, soy-free
   margarine

1 1/2 tablespoons water, 1 1/2
   tablespoons oil, 1 teaspoon
   baking powder; mixed together

1 teaspoon vanilla extract

1 tablespoon water

1 cup flour

1/2 teaspoon baking soda

1/2 teaspoon baking powder

1/2 teaspoon salt

1 cup quick oats

Preheat oven to 350°. Grease cookie sheets well. Cream together the sugars and margarine. Add water, oil, and baking powder mixture; beat well. Add vanilla and water; beat until smooth. Sift together the flour, baking soda, baking powder, and salt and add to wet ingredients.

Mix until smooth, then add oats. Mix well. Drop by teaspoonfuls, 2 inches apart, onto cookie sheet. Bake 10 minutes or until lightly browned. Immediately remove cookies to cooling racks.

Suggestions: Add 3/4 cup raisins. Or add 1/4 cup cocoa and 1/4 cup pecans, if allowed, to make chocolate nut oatmeal cookies.

Gingersnap Cookies

◆M◆◆E◆◆P◆◆S◆◆N◆

3/4 cup milk-free, soy-free
   margarine

1 cup brown sugar

1/4 cup molasses

2 tablespoons orange juice

2 1/4 cups flour

2 teaspoons baking soda

1/2 teaspoon salt

1 teaspoon ground ginger

1 teaspoon ground cinnamon

1 teaspoon ground cloves

granulated sugar

Preheat oven to 375°. Grease cookie sheets. Cream the margarine, brown sugar, molasses, and orange juice. In a separate bowl, sift together flour, baking soda, salt, ginger, cinnamon, and cloves. Stir the dry ingredients into the molasses mixture.

Form into small balls. Roll in granulated sugar; place 2 inches apart on greased cookie sheets. Bake for 12 minutes. Makes about 5 dozen cookies.

Pastel Melt Away Cookies

◆M◆E◆P◆S◆N◆

1/2 cup confectioners sugar
3/4 cup milk-free, soy-free
   margarine

1 cup flour
1/2 cup cornstarch

Beat confectioners sugar and margarine until light. Stir in flour and cornstarch. Refrigerate 30 minutes.

Preheat oven to 325°. Shape dough into 3/4-inch balls. Place 2 inches apart on ungreased cookie sheets. Bake for 10 to 13 minutes or until edges are lightly browned. Remove immediately and cool. Drizzle with glaze (recipe below). Makes 18 cookies.

Note: These cookies freeze well.

Glaze

◆M◆E◆W◆P◆S◆N◆

1 1/2 cups confectioners sugar
1 tablespoon milk-free, soy-free
   margarine

1 teaspoon vanilla extract
2 tablespoons orange juice
food coloring of your choice

Combine all ingredients in a small self-closing plastic bag. Blend together by kneading the bag. Slit corner of bag and drizzle glaze on cooled cookies.

Note: Add more orange juice if necessary.

—Cynde Sawyer

Old-Fashioned Cookies

◆Ⓔ◆Ⓢ◆

1 cup milk-free, soy-free margarine,
   softened
2 cups firmly packed brown sugar
3 tablespoons oil, 3 tablespoons water,
   2 teaspoons baking powder;
   mixed together

1 teaspoon vanilla extract
3 1/2 cups flour
1 teaspoon baking soda
1/2 teaspoon salt

Beat margarine at medium speed with an electric mixer. Add brown sugar, and beat well; set aside. Add wet ingredients; mix well. Combine flour, baking soda, and salt; add to creamed mixture, and mix well. Shape dough into two 16-inch rolls; wrap in waxed paper and chill at least 4 hours.

Preheat oven to 375°. Unwrap dough and cut into slices; place on ungreased cookie sheets. Bake for 6 to 8 minutes. Cool on wire racks. Yield: 8 dozen.

Note: This dough freezes well. Slice dough while frozen, then bake.

Fruity Cookies

◆Ⓔ◆◆◆◆

3 bananas
1 cup chopped dates
1/3 cup oil

1 teaspoon vanilla extract
1/2 teaspoon salt
2 cups rolled oats

Preheat oven to 350°. Grease cookie sheet. Mash bananas. Add dates, oil, and vanilla to bananas, and mix with a fork. Add remaining ingredients and let stand a few minutes for oats to absorb moisture. Drop by teaspoonfuls on cookie sheet. Bake 25 minutes or until nicely browned. Cool before removing from cookie sheet.

Suggestion: Add cinnamon, nutmeg, or allspice.

—Kathie Brough

Russian Tea Cookies

◆M◆E◆P◆S◆N◆

1 cup milk-free, soy-free
  margarine
1/4 cup sugar

1 teaspoon vanilla extract
2 cups flour
confectioners sugar

Preheat oven to 300°. Cream margarine and sugar. Add vanilla, then flour. Blend thoroughly. Shape into balls the size of large marbles. Place on cookie sheet and bake for about 20 minutes. Let cool. Roll in confectioners sugar. Store in air-tight container. Makes 3 dozen.

—Janice Berger

Holiday Cut-Out Cookies

◆M◆E◆P◆S◆N◆

2/3 cup shortening
3/4 cup sugar
1 teaspoon vanilla extract
1 1/2 tablespoons water, 1 1/2 tablespoons oil, 1 teaspoon baking
  powder; combined

4 teaspoons water
food coloring
2 cups sifted flour
1 1/2 teaspoons baking soda
1/4 teaspoon salt

Cream together shortening, sugar, and vanilla. Add water, oil, and baking powder mixture; beat until light and fluffy. Add food coloring as desired to remaining water (red and yellow for orange pumpkins, green for Christmas trees, and so on). Stir water into shortening mixture. Sift together dry ingredients; blend into creamed mixture. Divide dough in half. Chill 1 hour.

Preheat oven to 375°. Grease cookie sheets. On lightly floured board, using half of the chilled dough at a time, roll to 1/8-inch thickness. Cut in desired shapes with cookie cutters. Bake for 6 to 8 minutes. Cool slightly; remove from pan and continue cooling on wire racks. Makes 2 dozen cookies.

—Amy Rosenberg

Brett's Gingerbread Men

◆M◆◆E◆◆W◆◆P◆◆S◆◆N◆

1/4 cup milk-free, soy-free
   margarine
1/2 cup sugar
1/2 cup molasses
1 1/4 cups rye flour
1/2 teaspoon salt

1 1/4 cups cornstarch
1 teaspoon baking soda
1/4 teaspoon ground cloves
3/4 teaspoon ground cinnamon
1/4 teaspoon ground ginger
1/2 cup hot water

Preheat oven to 375°. Grease cookie sheets. Cream margarine with sugar, then add molasses; set aside. Sift together dry ingredients. Combine dry ingredients with water; add to creamed mixture. If dough is too gummy, add more rye flour. Roll dough on floured surface to 1/4-inch thickness. Cut out gingerbread men and decorate. Bake on cookie sheet for 12 minutes. When cooled, use icing to make mustache, boots, and gloves.

Note: These can be made into round cookies, too. Roll dough into walnut-size balls and flatten. Bake on greased cookie sheet for 8 to 10 minutes.

—*Cynde Sawyer*

Fudge Balls

◆M◆◆E◆◆W◆◆P◆◆N◆

2 cups sugar
1/2 cup Prosobee infant formula
1 stick milk-free margarine
1/2 cup unsweetened cocoa powder

1 teaspoon vanilla extract
3 cups quick oats
confectioners sugar

In a saucepan, combine sugar, infant formula, margarine, and cocoa; cook over medium heat for approximately 5 minutes or until mixture boils.

Remove from heat and add vanilla. Pour mixture over oats. Mix well and let cool. Form into small balls and roll in confectioners sugar. Makes approximately 48 fudge balls.

Rice Krispies Treats

◆M◆E◆W◆P◆S◆N◆

1/4 cup milk-free, soy-free margarine
1 package regular size milk-free,
 egg-free marshmallows

6 cups Kellogg's Rice Krispies cereal

Grease an 11x17-inch baking dish. Melt the margarine in a large pot over low heat. Add marshmallows and stir until completely melted. Remove from the heat and add Rice Krispies. Stir until the mixture is well coated. Pour into baking dish and flatten with the back of a spoon. Let cool before cutting into bars.

Suggestion: To make an Easter bunny, shape approximately 3 cups of the mixture into a ball to form the body. Make a smaller ball for the head, using approximately 2 cups.

Form the remaining cup of mixture into a ball to make the tail. Roll the tail in shredded coconut to give your Easter bunny a "cotton tail." Attach the head and tail to the body with toothpicks. Cut ears from pink construction paper and gently push them into the head. Cut whiskers from black construction paper, dip the ends in honey, and attach them to the face.

Notes: Be sure to remove the toothpicks before eating the bunny. Shape the mixture into an Easter basket or birthday basket to fill with treats.

Puffed Rice Treats

◆M◆E◆W◆P◆S◆N◆

milk-free, soy-free margarine
 (to grease pan)
1/4 cup milk-free, soy-free
 margarine

40 regular-size milk-free, egg-free
 marshmallows
5 cups puffed rice cereal

Grease an 8x8x2-inch pan with margarine. In a deep saucepan or pot over low heat, melt the margarine. Add the marshmallows; stir until melted. Remove from heat. Add the puffed rice and stir until completely coated. Press into pan. Allow to cool, then cut into squares.

◆ Milk-Free ◆ Egg-Free ◆ Wheat-Free

Caramel Popcorn

◆M◆E◆W◆P◆S◆N◆

1/2 cup popping corn
1 3/4 cups honey
1/4 cup milk-free, soy-free margarine

1/3 cup water
1/4 teaspoon salt

Pop the popping corn. Set aside. Grease cookie sheets. Combine the remaining ingredients in a saucepan and bring to a boil over medium heat, stirring continuously. Continue cooking, stirring occasionally, until mixture reaches 280° (use a candy thermometer). Pour caramel mixture over popcorn, and stir until well coated. Spread on greased cookie sheets to cool.

Note: To make caramel popcorn balls, grease your hands and form mixture into balls while warm. Wrap in waxed paper to cool.

Pretzels

◆M◆E◆P◆S◆N◆

1 tablespoon yeast
1/2 cup warm water
1 teaspoon honey

1 teaspoon salt
1 1/2 cups flour

Preheat oven to 425°. Lightly grease cookie sheet. Combine all ingredients to make dough. Knead the dough until soft, 5 to 10 minutes. (It should be easy to handle. If not, add more flour.) Shape into traditional pretzel shapes, or other shapes such as letters or numbers. Place on cookie sheet and bake 10 minutes.

Fruit and Popcorn Snack

◆M◆E◆W◆P◆S◆N◆

6 cups popped popcorn
1/3 cup shredded coconut
2 tablespoons milk-free, soy-free margarine

1/4 cup honey
3/4 cup dried apricots
3/4 cup raisins

Preheat oven to 300°. Pour popcorn and coconut into a 13x9x2-inch baking pan. Melt the margarine and mix with honey. Pour the margarine-honey mixture over the popcorn. Mix thoroughly. Bake 20 minutes. Stir twice during baking to be sure popcorn mixture bakes evenly.

Cut apricots into small pieces and mix with raisins. After the popcorn mixture has cooled slightly, stir in the apricots and raisins. Makes about 6 cups.

Strawberry Squares

◆M◆ ◆E◆ ◆P◆ ◆S◆ ◆N◆

1 1/4 cups sifted flour
7/8 cup milk-free, soy-free
   margarine, melted
1 cup brown sugar

1 1/4 cups quick rolled oats
1/8 teaspoon salt
3/4 cup strawberry jam (or any other
   fruit preserve)

Preheat oven to 350°. Grease an 8-inch square pan. Mix all ingredients except jam together. Press half of mixture into greased pan. Cover with jam. Spread remaining mixture on top. Bake for 30 minutes. Cut into squares when cooled.

Apricot Bars

◆M◆ ◆E◆ ◆W◆ ◆P◆ ◆S◆ ◆N◆

2 cups quick oats
1 cup barley flour
1/3 cup brown sugar
1/2 teaspoon salt

3/4 cup oil
1/2 teaspoon baking soda
12 ounces apricot preserves or jelly

Preheat oven to 350°. Grease an 11x17-inch glass pan. Mix together all ingredients except preserves or jelly. Set aside 3/4 cup of the mixture. Press remaining mixture into pan. Bake 10 minutes. Remove from oven and top with preserves or jelly. Spread reserved 3/4 cup of mixture on top. Return to oven. Bake 20 to 25 minutes. Let cool completely and cut into bars.

Note: Barley flour can be replaced with wheat flour.

Raspberry Bars

◆M◆E◆P◆S◆N◆

1 1/2 cups flour
3/4 cup sugar
1 teaspoon baking powder
1 cup milk-free, soy-free margarine,
    chilled

1 1/2 cups quick-cooking rolled oats
1/2 cup flaked or shredded coconut
raspberry preserves

Preheat oven to 350°. Grease 8x8-inch baking pan; set aside. In medium bowl, combine flour, sugar, and baking powder. Cut in margarine. Add oats and coconut; mix until crumbly. Press half of mixture into prepared pan. Spoon raspberry preserves over crumb mixture. Sprinkle remaining crumb mixture over preserve layer. Bake 30 minutes or until lightly browned. Center may seem soft. Cool completely in pan on wire rack. Refrigerate 1 to 2 hours before cutting or serving.

Banana Bars

◆M◆E◆W◆P◆S◆N◆

6 tablespoons milk-free, soy-free
    margarine, softened
1 cup brown sugar, firmly
    packed
1 1/2 tablespoons water, 1 1/2 table-
    spoons oil, 1 teaspoon baking
    powder; mixed together

1/2 teaspoon vanilla extract
1 large banana, mashed
1 3/4 cups barley flour
1 1/2 teaspoons baking powder
1/2 teaspoon salt
1 cup raisins

Preheat oven to 350°. Grease a 9-inch square pan. In large bowl, beat margarine and brown sugar until creamy. Beat in water, oil, and baking powder mixture; vanilla extract; and banana. Set aside. In another bowl, stir together flour, baking powder, and salt; combine with margarine mixture. Blend thoroughly. Stir in raisins.

Spread batter evenly in baking pan. Bake 40 minutes or until cake tester inserted in center comes out clean. Let cool in pan before cutting. Store in refrigerator.

Applesauce Bars

◆Ⓜ◆Ⓔ◆Ⓟ◆Ⓢ◆Ⓝ◆

1/2 cup milk-free, soy-free
　margarine
1 cup sugar
1 cup applesauce
1 teaspoon baking soda

1/2 teaspoon salt
1/2 teaspoon nutmeg
1/2 teaspoon cinnamon
2 cups flour

Preheat oven to 350°. Grease a 9x13-inch pan. Cream together margarine and sugar in a large mixing bowl; add applesauce. Blend in baking soda, salt, nutmeg, cinnamon, and flour. Pour into prepared pan. Bake 25 minutes. Frost or glaze if desired.

Suggestion: Add 1 1/2 cups of raisins.

—Paula Clark

Granola

◆Ⓜ◆Ⓔ◆Ⓟ◆Ⓢ◆Ⓝ◆

42-ounce box quick-cooking oats
14-ounce bag coconut flakes
12-ounce jar wheat germ
2 cups light brown sugar, packed

1 teaspoon salt
1 cup water
1 cup oil
2 tablespoons vanilla extract

Preheat oven to 350°. In large bowl or plastic container, combine oats, coconut, wheat germ, sugar, and salt. Combine water, oil, and vanilla. Add oil mixture to oat mixture, and blend well. Spread granola in a thin layer on cookie sheets. Bake for 15 to 18 minutes (until a golden color). Turn out into large container and let cool. Store granola in airtight container and refrigerate. Granola can be kept in refrigerator for 1 month or can be frozen. Makes 12 cups.

Suggestions: To make a spiced variation, add 1 1/2 teaspoons ground cinnamon and 1 teaspoon ground nutmeg to oat mixture. Or stir in 1 1/2 cups raisins after granola is baked.

Alissa's Frosted Apple Cookies

◆M◆E◆P◆S◆N◆

1/2 cup milk-free, soy-free
  margarine, softened
1 1/3 cups brown sugar,
  firmly packed
1 1/2 tablespoons water, 1 1/2 tablespoons oil, 1 teaspoon baking
  powder; mixed together
2 cups flour

1 teaspoon baking soda
1 teaspoon ground cinnamon
1/2 teaspoon salt
1/2 teaspoon ground cloves
1/2 teaspoon ground nutmeg
1/4 cup apple juice
Apple Frosting (recipe below)

Preheat oven to 400°. Grease cookie sheets. In a large bowl, beat margarine and brown sugar until creamy. Stir in water, oil, and baking powder mixture. Set aside. In another bowl, stir together flour, baking soda, cinnamon, salt, cloves, and nutmeg. Combine the flour mixture with the margarine mixture. Add apple juice and mix well. Drop dough by level tablespoonfuls onto baking sheets. Bake 10 to 12 minutes. Transfer to cooling racks. Frost cookies with Apple Frosting while they're still slightly warm.

—Alissa Taylor

Apple Frosting

◆M◆E◆W◆P◆S◆N◆

2 tablespoons milk-free, soy-free
  margarine, softened
1 1/2 cups confectioners sugar

1/4 teaspoon vanilla extract
1/8 teaspoon salt
2 tablespoons apple juice

Beat the margarine and confectioners sugar until creamy. Add vanilla extract, salt, and apple juice; stir until frosting is a spread-able consistency. Add more apple juice if necessary.

—Alissa Taylor

Coconut Cookies

◆M◆E◆P◆S◆N◆

1/2 cup milk-free, soy-free margarine, softened	1/4 teaspoon grated orange peel
1/2 cup sugar	1/2 teaspoon vanilla extract
1 1/2 tablespoons water, 1 1/2 tablespoons oil, 1 teaspoon baking powder; mixed together	1 cup flour
	1/2 teaspoon baking powder
	1/8 teaspoon salt
	2/3 cup flaked or shredded coconut

In a large bowl, beat margarine and sugar until creamy. Add water, oil, and baking powder mixture; orange peel; and vanilla extract. Blend thoroughly and set aside. In another bowl, stir together flour, baking powder, and salt. Add to margarine mixture and blend well. Add coconut and mix together well. Cover and refrigerate about 2 hours.

Preheat oven to 375°. Grease cookie sheets. Drop dough by teaspoonfuls about 2 inches apart onto cookie sheets. Flatten each cookie. Bake 10 minutes or until lightly browned. Let cool for about a minute on cookie sheets; transfer to racks to cool completely. Makes about 2 dozen.

Note: Dough may appear soft before refrigeration.

Cinnamon Cookies

◆M◆E◆P◆S◆N◆

2 cups flour	1 cup sugar
1/8 teaspoon salt	1 1/2 tablespoons water, 1 1/2 tablespoons oil, 1 teaspoon baking powder; mixed together
2 1/2 teaspoons cinnamon	
1 cup milk-free, soy-free margarine, softened	

Preheat oven to 350°. Sift flour, salt, and cinnamon together. Set aside. Cream margarine and sugar; add water, oil, and baking powder mixture. Add the dry ingredients. The dough will be stiff. Form into small balls and drop onto ungreased cookie sheet. Flatten gently with your hand and criss-cross with a fork. Bake 9 minutes.

Suggestion: Frost the top of one cookie and place another on top of it to make sandwich cookies.

Chocolate Valentine's Day Cookies

M E P S N

1 cup milk-free, soy-free margarine softened	3 cups flour
3/4 cup light corn syrup	3/4 cup unsweetened cocoa powder
1/2 cup sugar	1/2 teaspoon baking powder
	1/4 teaspoon salt

Cream margarine in a large mixing bowl; gradually add corn syrup and sugar, and beat until smooth. Set aside. Combine remaining ingredients in a medium mixing bowl; stir well. Gradually add to creamed mixture and mix well. Shape dough into two rolls, 2 inches in diameter. Wrap in waxed paper and chill at least one hour.

Preheat oven to 400°. Remove dough from waxed paper and cut into 1/8-inch slices. Place slices 1 inch apart on ungreased cookie sheets. Bake 5 minutes. Cool on wire racks.

Suggestions: After baking, sprinkle powdered sugar on the cookies. Before baking, roll dough in crushed rice cereal for a crunchy chocolate cookie.

Marguerite's St. Patrick's Day Shamrocks

◆M◆E◆P◆S◆N◆

1/2 cup milk-free, soy-free margarine
   softened
1/4 cup sugar

1 1/2 cups flour
green food coloring

Preheat oven to 350°. In a mixing bowl, combine all ingredients except food coloring and stir until completely blended. Add 2 or 3 drops of green food coloring and stir again. Form the dough into large balls; drop onto cookie sheets and flatten. Use a knife to cut shamrock shapes out of dough. Bake cookies 8 minutes or until the edges begin to turn golden brown. Allow the cookies to cool before moving them to cooling racks. When completely cooled, top with Green Icing.

Suggestion: Omit food coloring and icing; sprinkle cookies with green decorator's sugar before baking.

Green Icing

◆M◆E◆W◆P◆S◆N◆

2 cups confectioners sugar
1/4 cup water

green food coloring

Mix confectioners sugar and water together. Add drops of food coloring until desired color is achieved. Frost cookies.

—*Marguerite Furlong*

◆ Milk-Free ◆ Egg-Free ◆ Wheat-Free

4th of July Cookies

◈M◈E◈P◈S◈N◈

1/2 cup milk-free, soy-free margarine
   softened
1/2 cup shortening
1 cup sugar
3 tablespoons water, 3 tablespoons oil,
   2 teaspoons baking powder;
   mixed together

1 tablespoon grated lemon rind
1 1/2 teaspoons vanilla extract
3 1/2 cups flour
1/2 teaspoon baking powder
1/2 teaspoon salt
1 cup confectioners sugar, sifted

Beat margarine and shortening together until soft and creamy. Add sugar; beat well. Add water, oil, and baking powder mixture; lemon rind; and vanilla extract. Mix well. Add flour, baking powder, and salt; mix well. Cover and chill 1 hour.

Preheat oven to 375°. Divide dough in half; store one portion in refrigerator. On a lightly floured surface, roll dough to 1/8-inch thickness. Cut with a 2 1/2-inch star-shaped cookie cutter and place on ungreased cookie sheets. Bake 7 to 8 minutes or until lightly browned; cool on cookie sheets. Remove to wire racks. Sprinkle generously with confectioners sugar.

Cherry-in-the-Middle Cookies

◈M◈E◈P◈S◈N◈

1 cup milk-free, soy-free
   margarine, softened
1 cup confectioners sugar
3 tablespoons water, 3 tablespoons oil,
   2 teaspoons baking powder;
   mixed together

1 teaspoon vanilla extract
2 tablespoons water
2 3/4 cups flour, sifted
2 teaspoons baking powder
1/4 teaspoon salt
48 maraschino cherries, drained*

Preheat oven to 375°. Lightly grease two large baking sheets. In a large mixing bowl, cream together the margarine and confectioners sugar. Add water, oil, and baking powder mixture. Add vanilla extract and water; beat until batter is smooth. Set aside. Sift the flour with the baking powder and salt. Gradually blend the flour mixture into the wet batter until smooth.

Drop rounded teaspoonfuls of batter about 2 inches apart onto the baking sheets. Place a cherry in the center of each cookie. Bake 10 minutes or until the cookies are brown around the edges. Remove from the oven. Let cookies cool for 2 to 3 minutes before transferring them to wire racks to cool completely.

*Milk-free chocolate chips may be substituted

Snowballs

1/2 cup milk-free, soy-free margarine softened	1 1/2 teaspoons vanilla extract
1/2 cup shortening	1 1/4 cups flour, sifted
1/4 cup sugar	1/8 teaspoon baking powder
	confectioners sugar

Preheat oven to 400°. Lightly grease two large baking sheets. In a large mixing bowl, cream together the margarine, shortening, and sugar. Beat in the vanilla extract. Sift the flour with the baking powder. Add the flour mixture to the batter, 1/4 cup at a time. Knead the mixture into a smooth dough. If the dough is sticky, add more flour, a little at a time, until it is easier to work. Pinch off small pieces of dough and roll into balls. Arrange the balls 1 inch apart on the baking sheets.

Bake about 10 minutes or until the cookies are golden brown. Remove from the oven. After the cookies have cooled a few minutes, roll them in confectioners sugar. Transfer cookies to wire racks to cool completely.

Laura's Christmas Cookies

◆M◆E◆P◆S◆N◆

1 cup milk-free, soy-free
 margarine
2/3 cup brown sugar
3 tablespoons water

1 teaspoon vanilla extract
2 1/2 cups flour
1/2 teaspoon salt
raspberry jam

Cream together margarine and brown sugar. Add water and vanilla extract. Add flour and salt. Cover and chill dough 3 to 4 hours.

Preheat oven to 350°. Grease cookie sheets. Roll dough into 1-inch balls. Press an indentation in each cookie and fill it with jam. Cover with a little more dough. Bake 8 to 10 minutes.

Note: These can be made without the jam and frosted or sprinkled with confectioners sugar.

—Diane Smith

Stained Glass Cookies

◆M◆E◆P◆S◆N◆

1 cup milk-free, soy-free margarine
 softened
1 1/2 cups confectioners sugar
1 1/2 tablespoons water, 1 1/2 tablespoons oil, 1 teaspoon baking
 powder; mixed together

1 1/2 teaspoons vanilla extract
2 1/2 cups flour
1 teaspoon baking soda
1 teaspoon cream of tartar
3 colors of food coloring

Mix thoroughly margarine; confectioners sugar; water, oil and baking powder mixture; and vanilla extract. Add flour, baking soda, and cream of tartar. Divide dough in half. Divide one half into three sections. Add a different food coloring to each of the three sections, leaving the larger portion uncolored. Cover and chill dough 2 hours.

Preheat oven to 375°. Grease cookie sheets. Roll plain half of dough 1/8-inch thick on lightly floured board. Cut into any desired shapes. Place on cookie sheets. Roll colored dough; cut out different shapes of "stained glass" to fit on top of each plain cookie shape. Bake 7 minutes or until golden brown on edges. Makes about 2 dozen cookies.

Chocolate Drop Cookies

M E P S N

1 1/4 cups milk-free, soy-free margarine, softened
2 cups sugar
3 tablespoons water, 3 tablespoons oil, 2 teaspoons baking powder; mixed together

2 teaspoons vanilla extract
2 cups flour
3/4 cup unsweetened cocoa powder
1 teaspoon baking soda
1/2 teaspoon salt

Preheat oven to 350°. Cream margarine and sugar until light and fluffy. Add wet ingredients. Set aside. Combine flour, cocoa, baking soda, and salt; gradually blend into creamed mixture. Drop by rounded teaspoonfuls onto ungreased cookie sheet. Bake 8 minutes. Cool on cookie sheet about 1 minute; transfer from cookie sheet to wire rack. Cool completely before eating. Makes 4 dozen cookies.

Note: These cookies freeze well.

Candy Cane Cookies

M E P S N

1/2 cup milk-free, soy-free margarine, softened
1/2 cup shortening
1 1/2 tablespoons water, 1 1/2 tablespoons oil, 1 teaspoon baking powder; mixed together

1 cup confectioners sugar
2 1/2 teaspoons vanilla extract
2 1/2 cups flour
1 teaspoon salt
3/4 teaspoon red food coloring

Preheat oven to 375°. Mix thoroughly margarine; shortening; water, oil, and baking powder mixture; confectioners sugar; and vanilla extract. Blend in flour and salt. Divide dough in half; blend food color into one half. Shape 1 teaspoon of red dough and 1 teaspoon of plain dough each into 4-inch ropes. Twist the ropes together.

Place on an ungreased baking sheet and curve the top of the dough to form the candy cane handle. Bake about 9 minutes or until very light brown. Remove from baking sheet and allow cookies to cool on wire racks. Makes about 4 dozen cookies.

Suggestion: Sprinkle confectioners sugar on the cookies while they are still warm.

Doughnut Holes

◆M◆E◆P◆S◆N◆

1/2 cup plus 2 tablespoons milk-free, soy-free margarine, softened
1 cup sugar
3 tablespoons water, 3 tablespoons oil, 2 teaspoons baking powder; mixed together

3 cups flour
4 1/2 teaspoons baking powder
1/2 teaspoon salt
1/2 teaspoon nutmeg
1 cup apple juice*

Preheat oven to 350°. Line mini muffin tins with paper liners. Blend margarine with sugar. Add the water, oil, and baking powder mixture; mix well. Set aside. Sift together flour, baking powder, salt, and nutmeg. Add to the margarine and sugar mixture. Blend in the apple juice, and mix together thoroughly. Fill muffin tins 2/3 full. Bake 15 minutes or until doughnut holes are golden brown.

Suggestion: Combine 1/2 cup sugar with 1/2 teaspoon cinnamon; set aside. Melt 6 tablespoons margarine. While doughnuts are still warm, roll them in the margarine, then roll them in cinnamon sugar.

*Water may be substituted for apple juice.

Birthday Brownies

◆M◆ ◆E◆ ◆W◆ ◆P◆ ◆S◆ ◆N◆

1/2 cup shortening, softened
1 cup sugar
2 1/4 cups rice flour
1/2 teaspoon salt
1 teaspoon xanthan gum*

3/4 cup unsweetened cocoa powder
2 1/2 teaspoons baking powder
1 teaspoon vanilla extract
1 cup water

Preheat oven to 375°. Grease a 13x9x3-inch pan. Cream shortening and sugar until light and fluffy. (Be sure it's fluffy.) Mix in dry ingredients. Add vanilla extract and water. Beat until well blended. Spread evenly in prepared pan. Bake 40 to 45 minutes.

Note: These brownies hold together better if you let them cool completely before cutting and serving.

*Available from Ener-G Foods or large health food stores.

Australian Honey Joys

◆M◆ ◆E◆ ◆W◆ ◆P◆ ◆S◆ ◆N◆

5 cups Rice Chex cereal*
6 tablespoons milk-free, soy-free
  margarine or oil

1/3 cup sugar
2 tablespoons honey

Preheat oven to 300°. Line muffin tin with paper or foil liners. Put Rice Chex cereal in a large bowl; set aside. In a medium-size pot, combine margarine or oil, sugar, and honey. Bring to a slow boil over medium heat, stirring constantly. Pour over cereal and stir well. Quickly place into muffin tins. Bake 4 minutes. Let cool completely before serving.

*Other crunchy cereals may be substituted, if allowed.

—Suzanne Gumley

Chocolate Pretzels

◆M◆E◆P◆S◆N◆

2/3 cup milk-free, soy-free margarine
  softened
1 cup sugar
2 teaspoons vanilla extract
3 tablespoons water, 3 tablespoons oil,
  2 teaspoons baking powder;
  mixed together

2 1/2 cups flour
1/2 cup unsweetened cocoa powder
1/2 teaspoon baking soda
1/4 teaspoon salt
confectioners sugar

Preheat oven to 350°. In large bowl cream margarine, sugar, and vanilla extract. Add water, oil, and baking powder mixture. Add remaining ingredients except confectioners sugar. Blend thoroughly. Cut dough into 24 pieces. Roll each piece into a 12-inch long strip. Shape strips into pretzel shapes on cookie sheet. Bake 8 minutes or until set. Cool slightly before moving to wire rack. Sprinkle with confectioners sugar.

Holiday Cookies

◆M◆E◆W◆P◆S◆N◆

1/2 cup milk-free, soy-free
  margarine
1/4 cup sugar
1 tablespoon water
1/4 teaspoon vanilla extract

1/8 teaspoon lemon extract
1 1/4 cups rice flour
1 teaspoon cornstarch
confectioners sugar

Preheat oven to 375°. Grease cookie sheets. Beat margarine until creamy. Add sugar; beat well. Stir in water, vanilla extract, and lemon extract. Add flour and cornstarch. Mix well.

Roll into balls and drop onto cookie sheets. Bake 6 to 7 minutes. (Cookies will not brown.) Remove cookies to wire racks to cool. Sprinkle with confectioners sugar or frost.

Robin's Nest Cookies

◆M◆E◆P◆S◆N◆

1 cup milk-free, soy-free margarine, softened

3/4 teaspoon vanilla extract

3/4 cup confectioners sugar

1 1/2 cups flour

1/4 cup cornstarch

1 to 1 1/2 cups flaked coconut

1/2 cup small blueberries

Preheat oven to 300°. Beat margarine and vanilla extract until creamy. Set aside. In another bowl, combine sugar, flour, and cornstarch. Add to margarine mixture; beat well. Chill dough 1 hour.

Preheat oven to 300°. Shape dough into 1-inch balls; roll in coconut. Place 1 inch apart on cookie sheets; flatten slightly with bottom of a glass. Gently press 2 to 3 blueberries into each cookie. Bake 25 minutes or until coconut is golden.

Marshmallow Treats

◆M◆E◆W◆P◆S◆N◆

1/2 cup milk-free, soy-free margarine

3 cups egg-free miniature marshmallows

3 cups puffed rice cereal

Grease 8 1/2 x 4 1/2 x 2 1/2-inch loaf pan. Melt margarine over low heat in a large pot. Slowly add marshmallows; stir until melted. Remove from heat and add puffed rice 1 cup at a time. Mix well after each addition. Spread in prepared pan. Refrigerate until well chilled. Cut into squares before serving.

—Mary Jane Dykes

Abe Lincoln's Hats

◆M◆E◆P◆S◆N◆

1 1/4 cups flour
1/2 teaspoon baking soda
1/2 cup milk-free, soy-free margarine, softened
1/2 cup brown sugar, firmly packed

1/4 cup white sugar
1 1/2 tablespoons water, 1 1/2 table- spoons oil, 1 teaspoon baking powder; mixed together
3 teaspoons vanilla extract

Preheat oven to 375°. In a large mixing bowl, stir together flour and baking soda. Add margarine and blend together. Add sugars and beat until well mixed. Add water, oil, and baking powder mixture and vanilla extract. Beat until well mixed.

Drop dough by rounded teaspoons onto ungreased cookie sheets. Bake 8 to 10 minutes or until cookies are golden brown. Immediately after baking, while cookies are still warm, use a butter knife to cut cookies into hat shapes. Crumble the excess cookie pieces and set aside. When cookies are completely cooled, frost with Fudge Frosting (page 174). Press excess cookie pieces into the hat's brim.

—Marguerite Furlong

Sweetheart Cookies

◆M◆E◆P◆S◆N◆

2 3/4 cups flour
1 teaspoon baking powder
1/2 teaspoon baking soda
1/4 teaspoon salt
1 1/2 cups sugar
1/2 cup milk-free, soy-free margarine, softened

1 1/2 tablespoons water, 1 1/2 table- spoons oil, 1 teaspoon baking powder; mixed together
1/3 cup lemon juice concentrate
1/4 cup water
confectioners sugar

Sift together flour, baking powder, baking soda, and salt; set aside. In large mixing bowl, beat sugar and margarine until fluffy. Add water, oil, and baking powder mixture. Gradually add dry ingredients. Add lemon juice concentrate and water, and mix well (dough will be soft). Cover and chill overnight in refrigerator.

Preheat oven to 375°. Grease cookie sheets. On well-floured surface, roll out dough, one third at a time, to 1/8-inch thickness; cut with floured heart-shaped cookie cutters. Place 1 inch apart on prepared cookie sheets.

Bake 8 to 10 minutes. Remove to wire racks to cool several minutes. Roll in confectioners sugar and place on wire rack until completely cooled.

Chocolate Snap Cookies

1/2 cup milk-free, soy-free margarine, softened

3/4 cup sugar

1 1/2 tablespoons water, 1 1/2 tablespoons oil, 1 teaspoon baking powder; mixed together

1 teaspoon vanilla extract

1 1/2 cups flour

1/3 cup unsweetened cocoa powder

1/2 teaspoon baking powder

1/2 teaspoon baking soda

1/4 teaspoon salt

confectioners sugar

In a large mixing bowl, beat margarine; sugar; water, oil, and baking powder mixture; and vanilla extract until light and fluffy. Set aside. In a small bowl, stir together flour, cocoa powder, baking powder, baking soda, and salt. Add to margarine mixture, blending well. Refrigerate 1 hour or until firm enough to roll.

Preheat oven to 350°. Grease cookie sheets. On a lightly floured board roll out dough to 1/4-inch thickness and cut out with your favorite cookie cutter. Place cookies on prepared cookie sheets. Bake 8 to 10 minutes or until set. Cool 1 minute on cookie sheet before moving to wire rack. Sprinkle cooled cookies with confectioners sugar.

Suggestion: Sprinkle with colored sugar before baking and omit confectioners sugar.

Pear Blondies

◆M◆E◆P◆S◆N◆

1 cup brown sugar, firmly packed
1/4 cup milk-free, soy-free
   margarine
1 1/2 tablespoons water, 1 1/2 tablespoons oil, 1 teaspoon baking
   powder; mixed together

1/2 teaspoon vanilla extract
1 1/2 cups flour
1/2 teaspoon baking powder
1/2 teaspoon salt
1 cup canned pears, drained and
   chopped

Preheat oven to 350°. Grease an 8-inch square pan. In a medium bowl, combine brown sugar; margarine; water, oil, and baking powder mixture; and vanilla extract. Set aside. In another bowl, mix together flour, baking powder, and salt. Combine wet mixture with dry mixture. Blend thoroughly. Add pears. Bake 45 to 50 minutes or until golden brown and a cake tester inserted in center comes out clean. Remove from oven and let cool completely on a wire rack.

Alphabet Cookies

◆M◆E◆P◆S◆N◆

2 1/4 cups flour
1/2 cup sugar
1 teaspoon baking powder
1 teaspoon grated lemon peel
1/4 teaspoon salt
2 tablespoons oil

2 tablespoons milk-free, soy-free
   margarine, melted
3 tablespoons water, 3 tablespoons
   oil, 2 teaspoons baking powder,
   mixed together
1/4 cup water

Preheat oven to 350°. Grease cookie sheets. In large bowl, mix together flour, sugar, baking powder, lemon peel, and salt. Add oil; margarine; water, oil, and baking powder mixture; and water. Mix until well blended. Pull small pieces of dough and roll into ropes on lightly floured work surface. Form each rope into a letter of the alphabet or a number. Place on prepared cookie sheets. Cook 18 minutes. Remove cookies to cooling rack.

Note: To make learning fun, frost the cookies different colors. Make your favorite plain frosting and divide into several dishes.

Add a few drops of a food coloring to each dish. Let your child help you decorate the cookies. Your child will be able to practice letters, numbers, and colors and eat the props!

Pumpkin Cookies

3 cups flour
1 tablespoon pumpkin pie spice
1 tablespoon ground ginger
1/2 teaspoon salt
1 cup milk-free, soy-free margarine

2 cups sugar
1 cup canned pumpkin
1 1/2 tablespoons water, 1 1/2 tablespoons oil, 1 teaspoon baking
powder; mixed together

Grease cookie sheet. In a medium bowl, combine flour, pumpkin pie spice, ginger, and salt; set aside. In large mixer bowl, cream margarine and sugar. Beat until fluffy. Add pumpkin and water, oil, and baking powder mixture. Mix well. Combine with dry ingredients and mix well. Cover. Chill in refrigerator until dough is firm, about 1 hour.

Preheat oven to 350°. Drop dough by rounded teaspoonfuls onto a cookie sheet. Flatten slightly. Create a "stem" with dough and press into top of cookie. Bake 16 minutes, or until lightly browned.

Cool on wire racks. Make pumpkin faces using Pumpkin Frosting (page 174).

Banana Oatmeal Cookies

3/4 cup shortening
1 cup brown sugar, firmly packed
1 1/2 tablespoons water, 1 1/2 tablespoons oil, 1 teaspoon baking
powder; mixed together
1 cup mashed bananas

1 1/2 cups flour
1 teaspoon salt
1 teaspoon cinnamon
1/2 teaspoon baking soda
1/4 teaspoon nutmeg
1 3/4 cups uncooked quick oats

Preheat oven to 350°. Grease a cookie sheet. Combine shortening and brown sugar in a large bowl. Beat at medium speed using electric mixer until well blended. Add water, oil, and baking powder mixture and mashed bananas. Beat until blended. Set aside.

Combine flour, salt, cinnamon, baking soda, and nutmeg. Stir into creamed mixture until blended. Add oats and stir completely.

Drop dough by rounded tablespoonfuls 2 inches apart onto cookie sheet. Bake 15 minutes or until set. Cool on cookie sheet before removing to wire rack. Frost with Banana Frosting (page 174).

Sandwich Cookies

◆M◆◆E◆◆P◆◆S◆◆N◆

2 1/3 cups flour	1 cup milk-free, soy-free margarine,
1 cup sugar	softened
1/2 cup banana (about 1 medium	1 teaspoon vanilla extract
banana) cut into 1/4 inch slices	1/4 teaspoon salt
	Frosting (recipe below)

Preheat oven to 350°. Grease cookie sheet. In large mixer bowl, combine all ingredients. Beat at low speed until well mixed. Shape dough into 1-inch balls. Place 2 inches apart on cookie sheets. Flatten cookies with bottom of glass dipped in flour. Bake 12 minutes, or until edges are lightly browned. Remove immediately, and cool completely on wire racks. Spread 1 tablespoon of frosting over half of the cookies. Top with remaining cookies.

Frosting

◆M◆◆E◆◆W◆◆P◆◆S◆◆N◆

3 cups confectioners sugar	1/3 cup milk-free, soy-free
3 tablespoons water	margarine, softened
	1 teaspoon vanilla extract

In small mixer bowl, combine all frosting ingredients. Beat at medium speed until light and fluffy. Add more water if necessary.

Gingerbread Cookies

◆M◆E◆P◆S◆N◆

1/2 cup milk-free, soy-free margarine, softened

2/3 cup sugar

1/4 cup molasses

1 1/2 tablespoons water, 1 1/2 tablespoons oil, 1 teaspoon baking powder; mixed together

2 cups flour

2 teaspoons baking soda

1 teaspoon ginger

1 teaspoon cinnamon

1/2 teaspoon mace

3 tablespoons sugar

Cream margarine. Add 2/3 cup sugar; beat until light and fluffy. Add molasses and water, oil, and baking powder mixture. Beat well and set aside. Combine flour and remaining ingredients except 3 tablespoons sugar. Add to creamed mixture. Stir until well blended. Divide dough in half, wrap in plastic wrap, and freeze 30 minutes.

Preheat oven to 350°. Grease cookie sheets. Shape all of the dough into 1-inch balls. Roll in remaining 3 tablespoons sugar. Place on prepared cookie sheets. Bake 10 minutes.

Dusted Chocolate Cookies

◆M◆E◆P◆S◆N◆

1/2 cup milk-free, soy-free margarine, softened

3/4 cup sugar

1 1/2 tablespoons water, 1 1/2 tablespoons oil, 1 teaspoon baking powder; mixed together

1 teaspoon vanilla extract

1 1/2 cups flour

1/3 cup unsweetened cocoa powder

1/2 teaspoon baking powder

1/2 teaspoon baking soda

1/4 teaspoon salt

confectioners sugar

Preheat oven to 325°. Cream margarine; sugar; water, oil, and baking powder mixture; and vanilla extract until fluffy. Set aside. Combine flour, cocoa, baking powder, baking soda, and salt. Add to creamed mixture; blend well.

Roll dough on lightly floured surface to 1/4-inch thickness. (If necessary, chill dough until firm enough to roll.) Cut shapes with cookie cutters. Place on ungreased cookie sheet. Bake 5 to 7 minutes. Cool 1 minute on cookie sheet, then remove to wire rack to cool completely. Sprinkle confectioners sugar over cookies.

Colorful Sprinkle Cookies

◆M◆◆E◆◆P◆◆S◆◆N◆

1 cup milk-free, soy-free margarine	1 teaspoon vanilla extract
1 cup sugar	2 1/2 cups flour
3 tablespoons water, 3 tablespoons oil, 2 teaspoons baking powder; mixed together	2 teaspoons baking powder
	1/2 teaspoon salt
	1/2 cup coconut flakes
	colored sugar or sprinkles

Preheat oven to 350°. Cream margarine and sugar in a bowl. Stir in water, oil, and baking powder mixture and vanilla extract. Set aside. Sift flour, baking powder, and salt together. Add to creamed mixture and stir. Add the coconut and mix well. Shape into small balls. Roll balls in colored sugar or sprinkles. Bake until lightly browned, 9 to 10 minutes.

Crunchy Shortbread Cookies

◆M◆◆E◆◆P◆◆S◆◆N◆

1 cup milk-free, soy-free margarine, softened	1 teaspoon vanilla extract
1 1/4 cups brown sugar, firmly packed	2 1/2 cups flour

In large bowl, beat margarine and brown sugar until creamy. Add vanilla extract. Gradually beat in flour; blend thoroughly. Form dough into a ball, wrap in plastic, and refrigerate 1 hour.

Preheat oven to 300°. Grease cookie sheets. On a lightly floured board, roll out dough to 1/4-inch thickness. Cut with cookie cutters. Place on cookie sheets. Bake 35 minutes or until firm. Transfer to racks and let cool. Decorate as desired with frosting.

Wafers

◆M◆E◆W◆P◆S◆N◆

1 cup milk-free, soy-free
  margarine
3/4 cup sugar
1 tablespoon vanilla extract
1 teaspoon ground nutmeg

1 1/2 tablespoons water, 1 1/2 tablespoons oil, 1 teaspoon baking
  powder; mixed together
3 1/4 cups barley flour
2 teaspoons cornstarch

Preheat oven to 350°. Beat margarine in a large bowl. Add sugar
and beat until fluffy. Add vanilla extract; nutmeg; and water, oil,
and baking powder mixture. Beat well. Add barley flour and cornstarch. Mix until well combined.

Roll dough on a lightly floured surface into a 12 x 9-inch rectangle. Cut into 3 x 1-inch wafers. Place on an ungreased cookie
sheet. Bake 10 to 12 minutes or until bottoms are lightly browned.
Transfer to a wire rack to cool completely; frost when cool.

Brown-edged Wafers

◆M◆E◆P◆S◆N◆

1/4 cup sugar
2 teaspoons grated lemon rind,
  divided
2 cups flour
2 teaspoons baking powder
1/2 teaspoon salt
1/2 cup shortening

1 cup sugar
1 1/2 tablespoons water, 1 1/2 tablespoons oil, 1 teaspoon baking
  powder; mixed together
1/2 teaspoon vanilla extract
1/2 cup water
1/4 cup lemon juice

Preheat oven to 375°. Grease a cookie sheet. In a large bowl,
blend 1/4 cup sugar and 1 teaspoon lemon rind. Add flour, baking powder, and salt. Set aside. In medium bowl, cream shortening and 1 cup of sugar. Add water, oil, and baking powder mixture;
remaining lemon rind; and vanilla extract. Beat until mixture is
light and fluffy. Combine with dry ingredients. Add water and
lemon juice. Blend until smooth. Dough will be very soft.

Drop dough by teaspoonfuls 2 inches apart onto cookie sheets;
keep in mounds. Bake 10 minutes or until edges of cookies are

light brown. Remove from cookie sheets and cool on wire racks.
Store in tightly covered container.

Sweet Pretzels

Ⓜ Ⓔ Ⓦ Ⓟ Ⓢ Ⓝ

3 cups barley flour
1 teaspoon baking powder
1/2 teaspoon baking soda
1/2 teaspoon salt
1/2 cup milk-free, soy-free
   margarine
1 cup sugar

1 1/2 tablespoons water, 1 1/2 tablespoons oil, 1 teaspoon baking
   powder; mixed together
1 teaspoon vanilla extract
2/3 cup water
green colored sugar

Stir together flour, baking powder, baking soda, and salt. In a large
bowl, beat together margarine and sugar until fluffy. Add water, oil,
and baking powder mixture and vanilla extract; beat well. Add
water and beat until well mixed. Cover and chill overnight.

Preheat oven to 425°. Divide dough in half. On a floured surface,
roll each half into a 10 x 5-inch rectangle. Cut into 5 x 1/2-inch
strips. Roll each strip into a rope. Shape each rope into a pretzel.
Place pretzels on an ungreased cookie sheet. Brush with water.
Sprinkle with green sugar. Bake 5 to 6 minutes or until done. Cool
on a wire rack.

Butterscotch Bars

Ⓜ Ⓔ Ⓦ Ⓟ Ⓢ Ⓝ

3 tablespoons milk-free, soy-free
   margarine
1/2 cup brown sugar, firmly
   packed

2 cups egg-free miniature
   marshmallows
4 cups Corn Chex cereal
2 cups cornflake cereal

Grease a 9-inch square baking pan; set aside. Melt margarine in
a large saucepan over medium heat. Add brown sugar and stir
well. Add marshmallows and cook, stirring constantly, until marshmallows melt. Remove from heat and quickly stir in cereals. Press
mixture evenly into prepared pan. Let cool 1 hour before serving.

Crispy Oatmeal Cookies

◆M◆E◆W◆P◆S◆N◆

4 tablespoons oil
1/2 cup sugar
1 cup crispy rice cereal
1 cup oat flour

1/2 teaspoon baking soda
4 teaspoons applesauce
2 tablespoons finely diced apple
   chunks

Preheat oven to 350°. In a large mixing bowl, mix all ingredients together. Drop by teaspoonfuls on an ungreased cookie sheet. Bake 10 to 12 minutes.

—Linda Johnson

Fudgie Chocolate Sugar Cookies

◆M◆E◆P◆S◆N◆

7 tablespoons unsweetened cocoa powder
1 cup milk-free, soy-free margarine,
   melted
1 1/2 tablespoons water, 1 1/2 tablespoons oil, 1 teaspoon baking
   powder; mixed together

1 cup sugar
1 teaspoon vanilla extract
2 cups flour
1 teaspoon baking soda
1/4 teaspoon salt
additional sugar

Combine cocoa and margarine; stir well. Add water, oil, and baking powder mixture and sugar. Add vanilla extract and stir until completely mixed. Add flour, baking soda, and salt. Refrigerate 30 minutes.

Preheat oven to 375°. Shape dough into 1-inch balls; roll in additional sugar. Place on ungreased cookie sheets. Bake 8 to 10 minutes or until set. Remove from cookie sheets to cool on wire racks.

Note: For a crispier cookie, flatten dough balls before baking.

Halloween Cookies

◆M◆E◆P◆S◆N◆

1 cup milk-free, soy-free margarine	2 teaspoons baking powder
2 cups sugar	2 teaspoons baking soda
2 cups canned pumpkin	2 teaspoons cinnamon
1 teaspoon salt	4 cups flour
	Orange Icing (recipe below)

Preheat oven to 350°. Grease a cookie sheet. In a large bowl, cream together margarine and sugar. Add pumpkin. Mix well and set aside. In another bowl, sift together dry ingredients. Combine with sugar and margarine mixture. Blend well. Drop onto prepared cookie sheet by spoonfuls. Bake 10 to 12 minutes. When cool, top with orange icing.

Orange Icing

◆M◆E◆W◆P◆S◆N◆

1 pound confectioners sugar	1/8 teaspoon salt
1/2 cup milk-free, soy-free margarine	4 1/2 tablespoons orange juice
	1 1/2 tablespoons grated orange rind

Combine confectioners sugar, margarine, salt, and orange juice on top of double boiler on low heat. Simmer and blend until smooth. Remove from heat, add orange rind, and stir until thick. Frost cookies while icing is still warm. (Icing becomes firm after cooling.)

—*Carole Stull*

Old-Fashioned Holiday Cookies

◆M◆E◆P◆S◆N◆

1 cup milk-free, soy-free margarine, softened

2 cups white sugar

1/4 cup brown sugar, firmly packed

6 tablespoons water

2 teaspoons vanilla extract

3 tablespoons water, 3 tablespoons oil, 2 teaspoons baking powder; mixed together

4 cups flour

2 teaspoons baking powder

1/2 teaspoon salt

In a bowl, cream margarine and sugars until light and fluffy. Add water; vanilla extract; and water, oil, and baking powder mixture. Mix well. Add dry ingredients, and stir well. Cover and chill 1 hour.

Preheat oven to 350°. Grease two baking sheets; set aside. Roll out dough on a lightly floured surface. Cut dough with cookie cutters. Bake 10 to 12 minutes. Serve plain or frosted.

Molasses Cookies

◆M◆E◆W◆P◆S◆N◆

3/4 cup shortening

1 cup brown sugar, firmly packed

1 1/2 tablespoons water, 1 1/2 tablespoons oil, 1 teaspoon baking powder; mixed together

1/4 cup molasses

2 1/4 cups barley flour

2 teaspoons baking soda

1/2 teaspoon salt

1 teaspoon ground cinnamon

1 teaspoon ground ginger

1/2 teaspoon ground cloves

1/2 cup sugar

Beat together shortening and brown sugar until soft and creamy. Add water, oil, and baking powder mixture and molasses. Mix well and set aside. Combine flour, baking soda, salt, cinnamon, ginger, and cloves. Add to shortening mixture. Mix well. Cover and chill 2 hours.

Preheat oven to 350°. Grease two cookie sheets; set aside. Shape dough into 1-inch balls; roll balls in remaining sugar. Place on cookie sheets. Bake 12 minutes. Move to wire racks to cool.

◆ Milk-Free ◆ Egg-Free ◆ Wheat-Free

Shortbread Crescents

◆M◆E◆P◆S◆N◆

3 cups plus 3 tablespoons flour

3 tablespoons plus 1 teaspoon
cornstarch

1/2 teaspoon baking powder

1/2 teaspoon baking soda

1/4 teaspoon cream of tartar

1/4 teaspoon salt

1/4 teaspoon grated nutmeg

1 1/2 cups milk-free, soy-free
margarine, softened

2/3 cup confectioners sugar

1 1/4 teaspoons vanilla extract

2 cups confectioners sugar

Preheat oven to 350°. Line two cookie sheets with wax paper or parchment paper; set aside. In a large bowl, combine flour, cornstarch, baking powder, baking soda, cream of tartar, salt, and nutmeg. Set aside. In another bowl, stir together margarine, 2/3 cup confectioners sugar, and vanilla extract. Add half of the dry mixture to margarine mixture. Blend well. Add the rest of the dry mixture, and blend well.

Form a teaspoon of dough into a log, then shape the log into a crescent. Place on cookie sheet. Bake 14 minutes. Cookies will be a pale color. Cool 1 minute on cookie sheet. Transfer to cooling racks. Cool for 5 minutes. While still warm, drag cookies in confectioners sugar.

Creamy Sandwich Cookies

◆M◆E◆P◆S◆N◆

3/4 cup brown sugar, firmly packed
1 cup milk-free, soy-free margarine, softened

1 1/2 tablespoons water, 1 1/2 tablespoons oil, 1 teaspoon baking powder; mixed together
2 cups flour

Preheat oven to 325°. In large bowl, beat sugar and margarine until light and fluffy. Add water, oil, and baking powder mixture and blend well. Add flour; mix well. If dough is sticky, cover and chill 15 minutes.

Shape dough into 1-inch balls. Place 2 inches apart on ungreased cookie sheets. Flatten with bottom of glass dipped in flour. Bake approximately 12 minutes or until light golden color. Cool on wire rack.

Filling

2 tablespoons milk-free, soy-free margarine
4 tablespoons water

1 1/4 cups confectioners sugar
1/2 teaspoon vanilla extract

Heat margarine in saucepan over medium heat until light golden brown. Remove from heat. Stir in remaining ingredients, adding water to achieve desired consistency. Frost half of the cookies with the filling; top with remaining cookies.

Holiday Slices

◆M◆E◆P◆S◆N◆

6 tablespoons milk-free, soy-free margarine

1/3 cup shortening

3/4 cup sugar

1 1/2 teaspoons baking powder

1/2 teaspoon salt

1 tablespoon orange juice

1 1/2 tablespoons water, 1 1/2 tablespoons oil, 1 teaspoon baking powder; mixed together

1 teaspoon vanilla extract

2 cups flour

red food coloring

water

coarse green sugar

In a large mixing bowl, beat margarine and shortening until fluffy. Add sugar, baking powder, and salt. Beat well. Add orange juice; water, oil, and baking powder mixture; and vanilla extract. Stir well. Add flour and blend well. Turn dough onto waxed paper and knead in enough red food coloring for desired color. Cover and chill dough 2 hours.

Preheat oven to 375°. Roll half the dough at a time on a floured surface to 1/4-inch thickness. Cut into 3-inch rounds. Cut rounds in half. Brush water on rounded edge and in a 1/4-inch wide strip on top of cookie along the rounded edge. Dip edge in green sugar. Place on an ungreased cookie sheet. Bake 6 minutes or until lightly browned on bottom. Let cool.

Cocoa-Gingerbread Cookies

◆M◆E◆P◆S◆N◆

1/2 cup milk-free, soy-free margarine, softened	3 cups flour
3/4 cup sugar	2 tablespoons unsweetened cocoa powder
1 1/2 tablespoons water, 1 1/2 tablespoons oil, 1 teaspoon baking powder; mixed together	1 teaspoon baking soda
	1 teaspoon ground cinnamon
	1/2 teaspoon salt
1/2 cup molasses	1/2 teaspoon baking powder

In a medium bowl, beat margarine and sugar until creamy. Add water, oil, and baking powder mixture and molasses. Beat well. Set aside. In another bowl combine flour, cocoa powder, baking soda, cinnamon, salt, and baking powder. Gradually add to margarine mixture. Stir well. Divide dough in half and chill 1 hour.

Preheat oven to 350°. Grease baking sheets; set aside. On a lightly floured surface, roll dough, half at a time, to 1/8-inch thickness. Cut with cookie cutters. Place on baking sheets. Bake 6 minutes and cool on wire racks.

Zebra Cookies

◆M◆E◆P◆S◆N◆

1/2 cup milk-free, soy-free margarine, softened	1 1/2 tablespoons water, 1 1/2 tablespoons oil, 1 teaspoon baking powder; mixed together
1 cup sugar	
2 teaspoons baking powder	2 cups flour
1/4 teaspoon salt	3 tablespoons unsweetened cocoa powder mixed with 1 tablespoon oil
2 tablespoons water	
1 1/2 teaspoons vanilla extract	

In a large mixing bowl, beat together margarine and sugar. Add baking powder and salt; beat well. Stir in water; vanilla extract; and water, oil, and baking powder mixture. Add flour. Stir well. Divide dough in half. Into one half, stir cocoa and oil mixture. You will have one chocolate and one vanilla dough batter. Divide each portion in half to make four portions.

Using lightly floured wax paper, roll each portion into a 9x5-inch rectangle, about 1/4 inch thick. Carefully place a rolled-out plain dough rectangle on top of a chocolate rectangle; pat firmly. Starting at short end of rectangle, roll dough, using wax paper to help hold the dough together. Repeat with remaining dough. Wrap in plastic and chill 1 hour.

Preheat oven to 350°. Grease cookie sheet; set aside. Cut dough into 1/4-inch slices. Place 1 inch apart on a cookie sheet. Bake 9 minutes or until bottoms are lightly browned. Cool on wire rack.

George Washington's Cherry Cookies

◆M◆E◆P◆S◆N◆

1/2 cup milk-free, soy-free margarine, softened

1/2 cup sugar

1 1/2 tablespoons oil, 1 1/2 tablespoons water, 1 teaspoon baking powder; mixed together

1/2 teaspoon vanilla extract

1 cup flour

1/4 cup unsweetened cocoa powder

1/2 cup maraschino cherries, cut up

Preheat oven to 350°. Grease cookie sheets. Blend together margarine and sugar. Stir in oil, water, and baking powder mixture and vanilla extract. Add flour and cocoa powder. Mix thoroughly. Stir in cherries. Drop dough by teaspoonfuls 1 inch apart onto cookie sheet. Bake 15 minutes or until cookies become firm.

Lunchbox Cookies

1/2 cup brown sugar, firmly packed
1/2 cup confectioners sugar
1/2 cup milk-free, soy-free margarine, softened
1/2 cup shortening
1/2 teaspoon vanilla extract
1 1/2 tablespoons water, 1 1/2 table-spoons oil, 1 teaspoon baking powder; mixed together

2 1/4 cups flour
1/2 teaspoon baking soda
1/2 teaspoon salt
1/2 teaspoon cream of tartar
1/4 cup white sugar

Preheat oven to 350°. In a large bowl, combine brown sugar, confectioners sugar, margarine, and shortening. Beat until light and fluffy. Add vanilla extract and water, oil, and baking powder mixture. Blend well. Add flour, baking soda, salt, and cream of tartar. Blend until mixed well. Shape dough into balls; roll in remaining 1/4 cup sugar. Place 3 inches apart on ungreased cookie sheet. Flatten in crisscross pattern with a fork. Bake 10 to 14 minutes or until golden brown.

Baked Cinnamon Apples

6 medium apples
1 1/2 tablespoons lemon juice
5 tablespoons milk-free, soy-free margarine, softened
2/3 cup raisins

1/2 cup brown sugar, firmly packed
1/2 teaspoon cinnamon
1/4 teaspoon nutmeg
1/4 cup water

Preheat oven to 400°. Core apples, then peel off a 1/2-inch wide strip of peel around stem. Set apples upright in 9-inch square baking dish. Sprinkle with lemon juice and set aside. Thoroughly mix margarine, raisins, sugar, cinnamon, and nutmeg. Spoon mixture into apple centers. Distribute any remaining clumps in bottom of dish. Pour water into dish and cover tightly with foil.

Bake until apples are tender when pierced (35 to 45 minutes).

Milk-Free ◆ Egg-Free ◆ Wheat-Free

Serve warm; spoon any remaining sauce over apples in baking dish.

Note: This recipe works well with pears and peaches, too.

—Mary Jane Dykes

Vanilla Cookies

1 cup milk-free, soy-free margarine, softened
1 cup sugar
2 1/2 teaspoons vanilla extract
1/2 teaspoon ground cardamom

1/2 teaspoon salt
1 1/2 tablespoons oil, 1 1/2 table-spoons water, 1 teaspoon baking powder; mixed together
2 1/2 cups flour

Preheat oven to 375°. Combine margarine and sugar in a large bowl. Beat until light and fluffy. Beat in the vanilla extract; cardamom; salt; and oil, water, and baking powder mixture. Using a spoon, stir in the flour until well mixed.

Shape cookies into balls and drop onto cookie sheets. Flatten cookies, and bake until golden brown, about 10 minutes. Gently transfer cookies to wire racks. Sprinkle with colored sugar, if desired. Let cool before serving.

Note: This cookie dough can be packed into a cookie press to make different shapes.

Coconut Scones

2 cups flour
3/4 cup flaked coconut
2 tablespoons sugar
1 tablespoon baking powder

1/2 teaspoon salt
1/3 cup shortening
1 cup water
1/2 teaspoon vanilla extract

Preheat oven to 450°. Grease a cookie sheet. Set aside. In a large bowl, combine flour, coconut, sugar, baking powder, and salt. Cut in shortening until mixture resembles coarse crumbs. Set aside. Combine water and vanilla extract. Add to dry ingredients and stir well. Dough will be sticky. Drop dough by large spoonfuls onto the cookie sheet. Bake 10 minutes or until scones are golden brown.

Cookie Bars

◆M◆E◆P◆S◆N◆

1/3 cup milk-free, soy-free margarine, softened	1/2 teaspoon vanilla extract
1 cup sugar	1 1/4 cups flour
1 teaspoon baking powder, 1 tablespoon water, 1 tablespoon vinegar; mixed together	1 teaspoon baking powder
	1/4 teaspoon salt
1 banana, mashed	optional toppings: milk-free, egg-free marshmallows, fresh fruit, or colored sugar

Preheat oven to 350°. Grease and flour 13x9-inch pan; set aside. In a large bowl, beat margarine and sugar until light and fluffy. Add baking powder, water, and vinegar mixture; banana; and vanilla extract. Mix well. Add flour, baking powder, and salt. Pour batter into pan. Bake 25 minutes. Remove from oven. Sprinkle with desired topping and bake 10 minutes or until a cake tester inserted in center comes out clean. Cool in pan; cut into bars.

Suggestion: Be creative and add your own toppings to these cookie bars. They can also be served without a topping.

Gingersnap Oat Cookies

◆M◆E◆P◆S◆N◆

3/4 cup shortening	1 1/4 cups flour
1 cup brown sugar, firmly packed	1 tablespoon ground ginger
1/2 cup white sugar	1 1/2 teaspoons baking soda
1/2 cup molasses	1/2 teaspoon ground cinnamon
2 teaspoons vinegar	1/4 teaspoon ground cloves
3 tablespoons water, 3 tablespoons oil, 2 teaspoons baking powder; mixed together	2 3/4 cups quick oats
	1 1/2 cups raisins

Preheat oven to 350°. Grease cookie sheet. In a large bowl, combine shortening, sugars, molasses, and vinegar. Add water, oil,

◆ Milk-Free ◆ Egg-Free ◆ Wheat-Free

and baking powder mixture and beat until well blended. Set aside. In another bowl, combine flour, ginger, baking soda, cinnamon, and cloves. Mix into creamed mixture and stir until blended. Stir in oats and raisins. Drop by rounded teaspoonfuls 2 inches apart onto prepared cookie sheet. Bake 11 minutes. Cool on cookie sheet, then remove to cooling rack.

Tacky Snax

◆M◆E◆P◆S◆N◆

1 cup miniature milk-free, egg-free marshmallows	3/4 cup Cheerios cereal
	2 cups air-popped popcorn
1 cup small pretzels, broken up	1/2 cup tortilla chips
1 cup crispy rice cereal	1/2 cup raisins

Combine all ingredients in a large bowl. Stir well and serve as a snack. —*Mariel Furlong and Bethany Saunders*

Sticky Scones

◆M◆E◆P◆S◆N◆

2 cups flour	6 tablespoons water
2 tablespoons brown sugar	2 tablespoons dark corn syrup
2 teaspoons baking powder	2 tablespoons water, 2 tablespoons
1/4 teaspoon salt	oil, 1 teaspoon baking powder;
1/4 cup milk-free, soy-free margarine, chilled and cut into pieces	mixed together
	Cinnamon Syrup (page 130)

Preheat oven to 400°. Grease a cookie sheet and set aside. Combine flour, brown sugar, baking powder, and salt in a bowl. Cut in margarine until mixture resembles coarse meal. Set aside. In another bowl, combine water; corn syrup; and water, oil, and baking powder mixture. Add to dry ingredients, stirring just until dry ingredients are moistened (dough will be sticky).

Drop onto prepared baking sheet and form into 8-inch round shapes. Bake 15 minutes or until golden. Prepare Cinnamon Syrup. Pierce top of cooked scones with a fork. Drizzle hot syrup over scones. Cut into 12 wedges, and serve warm.

Cinnamon Syrup

◆M◆◆E◆◆W◆◆P◆◆S◆◆N◆

1/2 cup sugar

1/4 cup dark corn syrup

1/4 teaspoon ground cinnamon

1/2 cup water, divided

In a small saucepan, stir together sugar, corn syrup, cinnamon, and 1/4 cup water. Bring the mixture to a boil over medium-high heat, stirring constantly. Boil 2 minutes. Remove from heat and stir in remaining water. Let cool; transfer to a small pitcher.

Note: The syrup can be covered and stored in the refrigerator for up to a week.

Gingersnaps

◆M◆◆E◆◆P◆◆S◆◆N◆

3 cups flour

1 tablespoon baking soda

1 tablespoon powdered ginger

1/2 teaspoon cinnamon

2/3 cup oil

1 cup sugar

1/2 cup molasses

1 1/2 tablespoons water, 1 1/2 tablespoons oil, 1 teaspoon baking
powder; mixed together

1/2 cup water

Preheat oven to 350°. In a large bowl, mix together flour, baking soda, ginger, and cinnamon. Set aside. In another bowl, mix all remaining ingredients. Combine sugar mixture with flour mixture and mix well. Drop by tablespoonfuls onto ungreased cookie sheets. Bake 10 to 12 minutes.

—*Suzanne Gumley*

Iced Pumpkin Bars

◆M◆E◆P◆S◆N◆

1 1/2 cups flour
1 teaspoon baking powder
1 teaspoon pumpkin pie spice
1/2 teaspoon baking soda
1/2 teaspoon salt
1 cup canned pumpkin
3/4 cup sugar
2/3 cup oil

3 tablespoons water, 3 tablespoons
    oil, 2 teaspoons baking powder;
    mixed together
1/4 cup light brown sugar, firmly
    packed
2 tablespoons orange juice
1/2 cup crispy rice cereal
1/2 cup raisins
Icing (recipe below)

Preheat oven to 350°. Grease and flour a 13x9-inch baking dish; set aside. In a large mixing bowl, combine all ingredients except rice cereal and raisins. Beat at medium speed until smooth, scraping bowl frequently. Stir in cereal and raisins. Mix well. Pour into prepared pan. Bake 35 minutes or until a cake tester inserted in center comes out clean. Cool bars completely in pan on a wire rack. Top with icing.

Icing

◆M◆E◆W◆P◆S◆N◆

1 1/2 cups confectioners sugar
2 tablespoons orange juice

2 tablespoons milk-free, soy-free
    margarine, softened
1/2 teaspoon grated orange peel

Combine all icing ingredients. Beat at medium speed until smooth. Top pumpkin bars with icing.

Maple Crunchies

1/2 cup milk-free, soy-free margarine

2 cups flour

1 cup sugar

1 1/2 tablespoons oil, 1 1/2 tablespoons water, 1 teaspoon baking powder; mixed together

3 tablespoons pure maple syrup

1 1/2 teaspoons baking powder

1/2 teaspoon ground cinnamon

1/4 teaspoon baking soda

1/4 teaspoon ground mace

red and green coarse sugar in separate small bowls

Preheat oven to 350°. Grease cookie sheets. Set aside. Beat margarine in large mixing bowl. Add all ingredients except coarse sugar. Stir well. Form dough into 1-inch balls. Roll in coarse sugar. Place on cookie sheets about 2 1/2 inches apart. Bake 10 minutes or until set. Transfer to a wire rack to harden before serving.

Mourning Dove Cookies

1/3 cup milk-free, soy-free margarine

1/3 cup shortening

2 cups flour

3/4 cup sugar

1 1/2 tablespoons water, 1 1/2 tablespoons oil, 1 teaspoon baking powder; mixed together

1 tablespoon water

1 teaspoon baking powder

1 teaspoon vanilla extract

1/8 teaspoon salt

Beat margarine and shortening until softened. Add flour; mix well. Add all remaining ingredients. Beat well. Divide dough in half. Cover and chill 3 hours or until easy to handle.

Preheat oven to 375°. Roll each half of dough on a lightly floured surface to 1/4-inch thickness. Cut dough using dove-shaped cookie cutters. Place 1 inch apart on cookie sheet. Bake 7 to 8 minutes or until lightly browned around edges. Remove to cooling racks. Decorate with frosting or colored sugar.

Note: These can be made without cookie cutters. Roll into 1-inch balls and cook 15 minutes.

Chewy Bar Cookies

◆M◆E◆P◆S◆N◆

1/2 cup milk-free, soy-free
   margarine
1 cup firmly packed light brown sugar
1 cup firmly packed dark brown sugar
3 tablespoons oil, 3 tablespoons water,
   2 teaspoons baking powder; mixed
   together

1 1/2 cups flour
1 1/2 teaspoons baking powder
1/2 teaspoon salt
1 teaspoon vanilla extract

Preheat oven to 325°. Grease a 13x9x2-inch pan. Set aside.
Cream margarine and sugars. Add oil, water, and baking powder
mixture and beat well. Set aside. In another bowl, combine flour,
baking powder, and salt; add to creamed mixture. Mix well. Stir in
vanilla extract. Spread in prepared pan. Bake 30 minutes. Cut into
bars; cool before serving.

Suggestion: Drizzle allergy-free chocolate frosting over top of cookies.

Hermits

◆M◆E◆P◆S◆N◆

1/2 cup firmly packed brown sugar
1 1/2 tablespoons oil, 1 1/2 tablespoons
   water, 1 teaspoon baking powder;
   mixed together
1/4 teaspoon lemon extract
1/4 teaspoon vanilla extract
1/2 cup raisins

1 1/4 cups bread flour
1/4 teaspoon salt
1/2 teaspoon ground cinnamon
1/2 teaspoon ground allspice
1/2 teaspoon ground nutmeg
1/4 teaspoon ground cloves
1/2 cup shortening, melted

Preheat oven to 350°. Grease cookie sheets. Set aside. Combine
brown sugar and oil, water, and baking powder mixture; beat well.
Stir in lemon and vanilla extracts and raisins. Set aside. In another
bowl, combine flour, salt, and spices. Add to sugar mixture; stir
well. Add shortening; stir well. Drop dough by teaspoonfuls 2
inches apart onto cookie sheets. Flatten with a fork. Bake 12 minutes. Remove to wire racks to cool.

Annie's Granola Bars

◆M◆ ◆E◆ ◆P◆ ◆S◆ ◆N◆

1 1/4 cups firmly packed brown sugar	1 cup flour
1/4 cup milk-free, soy-free margarine, softened	1 teaspoon ground cinnamon
	1/2 teaspoon baking powder
2 tablespoons honey	1 cup quick-cooking rolled oats
1 1/2 tablespoons oil, 1 1/2 tablespoons water, 1 teaspoon baking powder; mixed together	1 cup toasted oat cereal
	1 cup raisins

Preheat oven to 350°. Grease a 13x9-inch pan. Set aside. In large bowl, combine brown sugar; margarine; honey; and oil, water, and baking powder mixture; beat well. Set aside. In another bowl mix flour, cinnamon, and baking powder; stir well. Add oats, cereal, and raisins. Combine with creamed mixture; stir well. Press mixture firmly into pan. Bake 30 minutes or until edges are light golden brown and center appears set. Cool completely. Cut into bars.

Chocolate Crisps

◆M◆ ◆E◆ ◆P◆ ◆S◆ ◆N◆

1/2 cup milk-free, soy-free margarine, softened	1 teaspoon vanilla extract
	1 1/2 cups flour
1 cup packed light brown sugar	1/3 cup unsweetened cocoa powder
1 1/2 tablespoons oil, 1 1/2 tablespoons water, 1 teaspoon baking powder; mixed together	1/2 teaspoon baking soda
	1 cup flaked coconut

Cream margarine and brown sugar in large bowl until blended well. Beat in oil, water, and baking powder mixture and vanilla extract. Set aside. In another bowl, combine flour, cocoa, and baking soda; mix well. Add to creamed mixture; blend until dough is stiff (it will be oily). Sprinkle coconut on work surface. Divide dough into 4 equal parts. Shape each part into a long, smooth roll. Roll in coconut until thickly coated. Wrap in plastic wrap; refrigerate until firm, at least 1 hour.

Preheat oven to 350°. Cut rolls into 1/8-inch-thick slices; place 2 inches apart on cookie sheets. Bake 10 minutes or until firm. Remove to wire racks to cool.

Funnel Cakes

(M)(E)(P)(S)(N)

3 tablespoons oil, 3 tablespoons water,
   2 teaspoons baking powder; mixed
   together
1 1/3 cups water
2 cups flour
4 teaspoons sugar

1/2 teaspoon salt
1 teaspoon baking powder
2 teaspoons baking soda
cooking oil
confectioners sugar

In a large bowl, combine oil, water, and baking powder mixture with water. Stir in flour, sugar, salt, baking powder, and baking soda. Mix until smooth. Set aside. Pour cooking oil 1/2-inch deep into a frying pan, and heat to 375° (use candy thermometer). Pour some batter in circle shapes into oil. Cook until light golden in color; turn once. Remove from oil and sprinkle generously with confectioners sugar while still warm. Repeat with remaining batter.

Old-Fashioned Oatmeal Cookies

(M)(E)(W)(P)(S)(N)

1/2 cup shortening
1/2 cup firmly packed dark brown sugar
1/2 cup sugar
3/4 teaspoon vanilla extract
1/2 cup rice flour

1/2 teaspoon salt
2 teaspoons baking powder
6 tablespoons water
2 cups quick oats

Preheat oven to 350°. Grease cookie sheets. Set aside. In a large bowl, cream shortening, sugars, and vanilla extract. Set aside. In another bowl, sift together rice flour, salt, and baking powder. Add to creamed mixture. Stir well. Add water and oats; mix well. Drop by teaspoonfuls onto baking sheet. Bake 10 minutes.

Vanilla Rainbow Cookies

Ⓜ Ⓔ Ⓟ Ⓢ Ⓝ

2 1/4 cups flour
1 teaspoon baking soda
1 teaspoon salt
1 cup milk-free, soy-free margarine, melted
3/4 cup sugar

3/4 cup firmly packed brown sugar
1 teaspoon vanilla extract
3 tablespoons water, 3 tablespoons oil, 2 teaspoons baking powder; mixed together
3 colors of coarse sugar

Preheat oven to 375°. In a large bowl, combine flour, baking soda, and salt. Set aside. In a mixing bowl, beat margarine, sugars, and vanilla extract until creamy. Add water, oil, and baking powder mixture. Blend well. Add to flour mixture. Blend well. Set aside. In a wide bowl or dish, combine colored sugars. Drop dough by rounded tablespoonfuls into sugar and roll until completely covered. Drop onto cookie sheets. Bake 9 minutes or until edges are golden brown. Let cool on cookie sheets 2 minutes. Remove and cool completely on wire racks.

Tropical Cookies

Ⓜ Ⓔ Ⓟ Ⓢ Ⓝ

1 cup flour
1/2 cup rolled oats
1/2 teaspoon baking powder
1/2 teaspoon baking soda
1/2 teaspoon salt
1 cup flaked coconut
1/4 cup milk-free, soy-free margarine, softened

1/2 cup sugar
1/2 cup light brown sugar, firmly packed
1 1/2 tablespoons water, 1 1/2 tablespoons oil, 1 teaspoon baking powder; mixed together
1 teaspoon vanilla extract

Preheat oven to 375°. Lightly grease two cookie sheets. Set aside. In a medium bowl, combine flour, oats, baking powder, baking soda, salt, and coconut. Mix well. Set aside. In a large bowl, cream margarine and the two sugars. Beat in water, oil, and baking powder mixture. Beat in vanilla extract. Gradually blend in the dry ingredients. Drop the dough by spoonfuls 1 1/2 inches apart onto prepared sheets. Bake 8 to 10 minutes until lightly colored. Cool on wire racks.

Yummy Crinkles Cookies

◆M◆E◆P◆S◆N◆

2 cups flour
2 teaspoons baking powder
1/2 cup oil
1 1/2 cups sugar
3 tablespoons water, 3 tablespoons oil,
   2 teaspoons baking powder; mixed
   together

1/2 cup plus 1 tablespoon
   unsweetened cocoa powder
3 tablespoons milk-free, soy-free
   margarine, melted
1/4 cup water
1 teaspoon vanilla extract
confectioners sugar

Preheat oven to 350°. Lightly grease two cookie sheets. Set aside. In large bowl, combine flour and baking powder. Set aside. In medium bowl, beat oil and sugar until well blended. Beat in the water, oil, and baking powder mixture. Add cocoa powder, margarine, water, and vanilla extract. Blend into dry ingredients. Pinch off quarter-size pieces of dough and roll into balls. Roll in confectioners sugar and place 1 1/2 inches apart on prepared baking sheets. Bake 14 minutes or until firm to the touch. Roll again in confectioners sugar while still warm. Cool on wire racks.

Chocolate Cookies

◆M◆E◆P◆S◆N◆

1 3/4 cups flour
2/3 cup sifted confectioners sugar
1/3 cup unsweetened cocoa powder
2 1/4 teaspoons baking powder
1/8 teaspoon salt
3 tablespoons oil
1 cup brown sugar, firmly packed

2 1/2 tablespoons light corn syrup
1 tablespoon water
2 1/2 teaspoons vanilla extract
4 1/2 tablespoons oil, 4 1/2 tablespoons water, 1 tablespoon
   baking powder; mixed together

Preheat oven to 350°. Grease cookie sheets. Set aside. In a large bowl, combine flour, confectioners sugar, cocoa powder, baking powder, and salt. Stir well. Set aside. In another bowl, combine oil, brown sugar, corn syrup, water, and vanilla extract. Add oil, water, and baking powder mixture. Stir well. Add to flour mixture. Blend well.

Drop dough by tablespoons 2 inches apart onto cookie sheets. Bake 8 minutes. Let cool until firm. Remove to wire racks.

Sweet Heart Cookies

◆M◆E◆P◆S◆N◆

1 cup shortening
1 1/2 cups brown sugar, firmly packed
3 tablespoons water, 3 tablespoons oil, 2 teaspoons baking powder; mixed together
2 teaspoons vanilla extract
2 cups flour

1 teaspoon baking powder
1 teaspoon salt
1/2 teaspoon baking soda
2 1/2 cups quick oats
12-ounce jar strawberry jam
sugar

In large mixing bowl, combine shortening and brown sugar. Beat until well blended. Add water, oil, and baking powder mixture and vanilla extract. Set aside. In medium bowl, combine flour, baking powder, salt, and baking soda. Mix into creamed mixture. Stir well. Stir in oats. Cover and refrigerate 1 hour.

Preheat oven to 350°. Grease cookie sheet. Set aside. On floured surface, roll out dough, half at a time, to 1/4-inch thickness. Cut out with floured heart-shaped cookie cutter. Place 1 teaspoonful of jam in center of a heart. Top with another heart. Press edges to seal. Prick centers. Sprinkle with sugar. Bake 12 to 15 minutes or until lightly browned. Cool 2 minutes on cookie sheet. Remove to cooling rack.

◆ Milk-Free ◆ Egg-Free ◆ Wheat-Free

Vanilla-Coconut Cookies

◆M◆E◆P◆S◆N◆

1/2 cup milk-free, soy-free margarine, softened

1 cup light brown sugar, firmly packed

1 1/2 tablespoons water, 1 1/2 tablespoons oil, 1 teaspoon baking powder; mixed together

1 1/4 cups flour

1/4 teaspoon baking powder

1/8 teaspoon baking soda

1/8 teaspoon salt

1/2 cup flaked coconut

Preheat oven to 350°. Grease cookie sheets and set aside. In large bowl, cream margarine and brown sugar. Add water, oil, and baking powder mixture; beat until fluffy. Set aside. In another bowl, combine flour, baking powder, baking soda, and salt. Stir into creamed mixture. Blend well. Stir in coconut. Drop dough by teaspoonfuls 2 inches apart onto prepared cookie sheets. Bake 10 minutes or until firm. Remove to wire racks to cool.

Sugar & Spice Cookies

◆M◆E◆P◆S◆N◆

3 cups flour

2 teaspoons baking powder

1/4 teaspoon salt

1 cup milk-free, soy-free margarine

1 1/3 cups sugar

3 tablespoons water, 3 tablespoons oil, 2 teaspoons baking powder; mixed together

1 teaspoon vanilla extract

3 tablespoons sugar

2 teaspoons ground cinnamon

Preheat oven to 350°. Lightly grease 2 cookie sheets. Set aside. In a large bowl, combine flour, baking powder, and salt. In another bowl, cream margarine and sugar. Beat in water, oil, and baking powder mixture; and vanilla extract. Gradually blend in the dry ingredients. Set aside. In a shallow dish, combine the sugar and cinnamon. Shape dough into 1-inch balls and roll in the cinnamon-sugar. Place 1 1/2 inches apart on prepared baking sheets. Bake 10 to 12 minutes, or until lightly colored. Cool on wire racks.

—*Mariel Furlong*

Friendship Cookies

◆M◆E◆P◆S◆N◆

1/3 cup brown sugar, firmly packed
1/4 cup sugar
1/2 cup shortening
1/2 teaspoon vanilla extract
1 1/2 tablespoons water, 1 1/2 tablespoons
   oil, 1 teaspoon baking powder; mixed
   together

1 1/4 cups flour
1/2 teaspoon baking soda
1/4 teaspoon salt

Preheat oven to 350°. Line large cookie sheet with foil; grease foil. Set aside. In large bowl, combine sugars and shortening; beat until light and fluffy. Add vanilla extract and water, oil, and baking powder mixture; blend well. Add flour, baking soda, and salt; mix well. Place dough in center of prepared cookie sheet. Press dough to 12-inch circle.

Bake 17 to 21 minutes or until slightly firm when touched in center. Cool completely. Decorate as desired with frosting. Cut into squares or allow each person to break off a piece.

Note: This makes a great substitute for a traditional birthday cake. It can also be a fun project for young children.

Chocolate Snickerdoodle Cookies

1 cup milk-free, soy-free margarine, softened	2 cups rolled oats
3/4 cup packed brown sugar	1 1/2 cups flour
3/4 cup sugar	1/4 cup unsweetened cocoa powder
3 tablespoons water, 3 tablespoons oil, 2 teaspoons baking powder; mixed together	1 teaspoon baking soda
	2 tablespoons sugar
	2 tablespoons cocoa
	2 tablespoons ground cinnamon

Preheat oven to 375°. Lightly grease cookie sheets. Set aside. Beat margarine, brown sugar, and 3/4 cup sugar in large bowl until light and fluffy. Add water, oil, and baking powder mixture; mix well. Set aside.

In a medium bowl, combine oats, flour, cocoa, and baking soda. Stir into margarine and sugar mixture until blended. Set aside. In a small bowl, mix the remaining 2 tablespoons sugar and cocoa with cinnamon. Drop dough by rounded teaspoonfuls into cinnamon mixture; toss to coat. Place 2 inches apart on prepared cookie sheets. Bake 8 to 10 minutes, or until firm in center. Do not overbake. Remove to wire racks to cool.

Stick Cookies

1 1/2 cups milk-free, soy-free margarine, softened	2 cups flour
1/2 cup confectioners sugar	1/4 cup water
1/2 teaspoon vanilla extract	colored sugar

Preheat the oven to 350°. Lightly grease two cookie sheets. Set aside. In a large bowl, cream margarine and confectioners sugar. Beat in vanilla extract. Gradually blend in flour and water. Pinch off quarter-size pieces of dough and roll into thin ropes about 8 inches long. Fold the ropes in half and twist them. Roll in colored sugar. Place 1 inch apart on prepared baking sheets. Bake 12 to 15 minutes, or until lightly colored. Cool on wire racks.

Nana Cookies

M E P S N

1 1/2 cups flour	1 cup sugar
1/2 teaspoon baking soda	1 1/2 tablespoons water, 1 1/2 table-
3/4 teaspoon ground cinnamon	spoons oil, 1 teaspoon baking
1/4 teaspoon ground nutmeg	powder; mixed together
1/4 teaspoon salt	2 bananas, mashed
3/4 cup shortening	1 3/4 cups rolled oats

Preheat oven to 400°. In a medium bowl, combine flour, baking soda, cinnamon, nutmeg, and salt. Set aside. In large bowl, cream shortening and sugar. Beat in water, oil, and baking powder mixture and bananas. Gradually blend in dry ingredients. Fold in oats. Drop dough by spoonfuls 1 1/2 inches apart onto cookie sheets. Bake 10 minutes or until lightly browned. Cool on wire racks.

Chocolate-Cherry Butter Ball Cookies

M E P S N

1 cup milk-free, soy-free margarine	1/4 cup unsweetened cocoa
1/2 cup plus 1 tablespoon confectioners	powder
sugar	3/4 cup drained maraschino cherries,
1 teaspoon vanilla extract	chopped
1 3/4 cups flour	1/4 cup flour

Preheat oven to 350°. In mixing bowl, cream together margarine and confectioners sugar until light and fluffy. Add vanilla extract and beat well. Add 1 3/4 cups flour and cocoa. Mix well. Set aside. Squeeze cherries with paper towels until cherries are dry. Fold cherries into dough. Add as much of the remaining 1/4 cup flour as needed to make dough fudge-like. Shape into balls and place on ungreased baking sheet. Bake 15 minutes.

Suggestion: For a white cookie, omit cocoa powder and add all of the 1/4 cup flour. Roll in confectioners sugar while still warm.

—*Marybeth Cave*

Cinnamon Bubbles

◆Ⓜ◆Ⓔ◆Ⓦ◆Ⓟ◆Ⓢ◆Ⓝ◆

1/2 cup milk-free, soy-free margarine	1 1/3 cups brown rice flour
3/4 cup sugar	1/2 teaspoon cream of tartar
1 1/2 tablespoons water, 1 1/2 tablespoons oil, 1 teaspoon baking powder; mixed together	1/4 teaspoon baking soda
	1/8 teaspoon salt
	1 tablespoon sugar
1/2 teaspoon vanilla extract	1 teaspoon cinnamon

Preheat oven to 400°. In a mixing bowl, cream together margarine and sugar. Beat in water, oil, and baking powder mixture and vanilla extract. Stir in flour, cream of tartar, baking soda, and salt. Mix well and set aside. In a small bowl, mix together sugar and cinnamon. Set aside. Shape dough into small balls. Roll each in sugar and cinnamon mixture. Place on ungreased baking sheets and bake 10 minutes.

—Teresa Homan

Vanilla Spritz Cookies

◆Ⓜ◆Ⓔ◆Ⓦ◆Ⓟ◆Ⓢ◆Ⓝ◆

1 cup milk-free, soy-free margarine	1 teaspoon vanilla extract
3/4 cup sugar	1 1/4 cups rice flour
1 1/2 tablespoons water, 1 1/2 tablespoons oil, 1 teaspoon baking powder; mixed together	1 1/2 cups oat flour
	1/2 teaspoon salt
	1/4 teaspoon baking powder

Preheat oven to 375°. Cream margarine and sugar well. Beat in water, oil, and baking powder mixture and vanilla extract. Set aside. In separate bowl, combine dry ingredients. Gradually blend dry ingredients into wet mixture. Texture should be soft and pliable. If dough is too soft, add a little flour to get the right consistency. If dough is stiff or crumbly, add a little applesauce or other moist ingredient of choice. Fill cookie press and form cookies on ungreased cookie sheets. Bake 10 minutes. Remove to cooling racks. Store in airtight container. These cookies freeze well.

—Kathy Lundquist

Crescent Cookies

1/2 cup milk-free, soy-free margarine, softened	1 cup barley flour
1/4 cup confectioners sugar	1 cup Rice Krispies cereal
1 teaspoon vanilla extract	confectioners sugar

Preheat oven to 350°. In a bowl, mix together margarine, confectioners sugar, and vanilla extract until blended. Gradually stir in flour and cereal. Shape dough into crescents or balls. Place on ungreased cookie sheets. Bake 10 minutes or until firm. Gently roll each cookie in confectioners sugar. Cool on wire racks.

Note: Cookies are crumbly when hot but firm up quickly.

—Kathy Lundquist

Sesame Sweethearts

1/2 cup milk-free, soy-free margarine, softened	2 teaspoons vanilla extract
1/2 cup sugar	2 cups flour
1 1/2 tablespoons water, 1 1/2 tablespoons oil, 1 teaspoon baking powder; mixed together	1/2 teaspoon baking powder
	1/4 teaspoon salt
	water
	sesame seeds

Preheat oven to 375°. Lightly grease two baking sheets; set aside. In a large bowl, beat margarine and sugar until light and fluffy. Beat in water, oil, and baking powder mixture and vanilla extract. Add flour, baking powder, and salt. Blend well. Roll dough out to 1/4-inch thickness. Cut out cookies with lightly floured heart-shaped cookie cutters. Place on prepared baking sheets. Brush cookies lightly with water, then sprinkle with sesame seeds. Bake 10 minutes or until firm. Cool completely on wire racks.

Snow White Cookies

◆M◆E◆P◆S◆N◆

1 1/2 cups flour
1 teaspoon baking powder
1/2 teaspoon salt
1/2 cup sugar
1/4 cup milk-free, soy-free margarine,
    softened

1 1/2 tablespoons water, 1 1/2 table-
    spoons oil, 1 teaspoon baking
    powder; mixed together
1 teaspoon vanilla extract
1/4 cup water
Snow White Frosting (recipe below)

Preheat oven to 350°. Grease several baking sheets. Set aside. In a small bowl, sift together flour, baking powder, and salt. Set aside. In a large bowl, combine sugar and margarine. Beat until fluffy. Add water, oil, and baking powder mixture and vanilla extract. Mix well. Add flour mixture and water. Stir until blended. Place a greased cookie cutter on a prepared baking sheet. Drop cookie dough into the cutter. Spread evenly to fill. Carefully remove the cookie cutter from dough. Leaving 3 inches between cookies, repeat with the remaining dough. Bake 10 to 12 minutes. Transfer to wire racks to cool completely. Frost with Snow White Frosting.

Snow White Frosting

◆M◆E◆W◆P◆S◆N◆

1 cup vegetable shortening
1/2 cup corn syrup

1/2 teaspoon vanilla extract
1 1/2 cups confectioners sugar

In a small bowl, combine shortening, corn syrup, and vanilla extract. Mix well. Add confectioners sugar. Blend until smooth and fluffy. Frost cookies.

Apple Fritters

◆M◆E◆P◆S◆N◆

oil

3 cups flour

1/2 teaspoon salt

2 teaspoons baking powder

1/2 cup sugar

1 1/2 tablespoons water, 1 1/2 tablespoons oil, 1/2 teaspoon baking
powder; mixed together

1 cup water

1/4 cup milk-free, soy-free
margarine, melted

2 teaspoons grated orange rind

1/4 cup orange juice

2 cups diced cooking apple

1 teaspoon vanilla extract

confectioners sugar

In a deep pot, pour oil to a depth of 2 inches. Set temperature to medium-high. In a large bowl, combine flour, salt, baking powder, and sugar. Stir and set aside. In a separate bowl, combine water, oil, and baking powder mixture; 1 cup water, and margarine. Stir well. Stir in orange rind, orange juice, apple, and vanilla extract. Add to flour mixture, stirring until just moistened. Drop batter by rounded tablespoonfuls into hot oil. When fritters are golden brown, turn once and fry the other side until golden brown. Remove and drain on paper towels. Sprinkle with confectioners sugar and serve.

Note: You may also bake these at 350° on a greased cookie sheet for 15 minutes.

Chocolate Fudge

◆M◆E◆P◆S◆N◆

3 cups flour
1 1/2 cups unsweetened cocoa powder
1/4 teaspoon salt
1/2 teaspoon cinnamon
3/4 pound (3 sticks) milk-free, soy-free margarine

2 1/2 cups sifted confectioners sugar
3 tablespoons oil, 3 tablespoons water, 2 teaspoons baking powder; mixed together
1 teaspoon vanilla extract

In a large bowl, sift together flour, cocoa, salt, and cinnamon. Set aside. In another bowl, cream margarine and sugar until fluffy. Beat in oil, water, and baking powder mixture and vanilla extract. Add flour mixture. Blend until thoroughly combined. Wrap dough in plastic; chill 1 hour. Roll out dough between two sheets of waxed paper to 1/2-inch thickness, and cut into squares.

Caramel Cookies

◆M◆E◆P◆S◆N◆

1/2 cup water
1/2 cup milk-free, soy-free margarine, softened
1 1/2 cups dark brown sugar, firmly packed

1 1/2 tablespoons water, 1 1/2 tablespoons oil, 1 teaspoon baking powder; mixed together
1 teaspoon vanilla extract
2 cups flour
1/2 teaspoon baking soda

Preheat oven to 375°. Grease two large baking sheets. Set aside. Heat water in microwave oven for 1 minute. Set aside. In a large mixing bowl, cream together margarine and brown sugar. Beat in water, oil, and baking powder mixture until the batter is light and creamy. Stir in warm water and vanilla extract. Set aside. In another bowl, sift flour with baking soda and fold into batter. Drop by rounded teaspoonfuls onto baking sheets, about 2 inches apart. Bake 15 minutes or until cookies have browned around the edges. Remove from oven. After cookies have started to cool, transfer to wire racks to cool completely.

Vanilla Cookies

◆M◆E◆W◆P◆S◆N

1 cup milk-free, soy-free margarine, softened
3 teaspoons liquid egg substitute
4 tablespoons water
3/4 cup brown sugar

3/4 cup sugar
1 teaspoon vanilla extract
2 3/4 cups oat flour
1 teaspoon salt
1 teaspoon baking soda

Preheat oven to 375°. In medium bowl, mix margarine, egg substitute, water, sugars, and vanilla extract until creamy. Set aside. In another bowl, stir together flour, salt, and baking soda until blended. Add to margarine mixture. Mix until combined. Drop by rounded spoonfuls onto baking sheets. Bake 9 minutes. Let cool before removing.

—Michelle Howard

Maple Cookies

◆M◆E◆P◆S◆N

2 1/4 cups flour
1 cup sugar
3/4 cup milk-free, soy-free margarine, softened
1 1/2 tablespoons water, 1 1/2 tablespoons oil, 1 teaspoon baking powder; mixed together

1 teaspoon pumpkin pie spice
1/2 teaspoon baking soda
1/2 teaspoon salt
3/4 cup applesauce
1 cup raisins

Preheat oven to 375°. Grease baking sheets and set aside. In large mixing bowl, combine all ingredients except raisins. Beat at low speed, scraping bowl often, until well blended. Stir in raisins. Drop by rounded spoonfuls onto prepared sheets and bake 10 minutes. Cool completely on wire racks.

◆ Milk-Free ◆ Egg-Free ◆ Wheat-Free

Raisin Bars

◆M◆E◆P◆S◆N◆

1 cup flour
1/4 cup sugar
1/3 cup milk-free, soy-free margarine
3 tablespoons water, 3 tablespoons oil,
   2 teaspoons baking powder; mixed
   together
1 cup sugar
2 tablespoons flour

1/2 teaspoon baking powder
1/4 teaspoon salt
1 teaspoon orange rind, grated
2 tablespoons orange juice
3/4 cup raisins, chopped
1/2 cup flaked coconut
Raising Bar Topping (recipe below)

Preheat oven to 350°. Lightly grease a 9-inch square pan; set aside. In a medium bowl, combine 1 cup flour and 1/4 cup sugar; cut in margarine with a pastry blender until mixture is crumbly. Press into bottom of prepared pan. In a separate bowl, combine all remaining ingredients. Stir until blended. Pour over crust. Bake 40 minutes.

Raisin Bar Topping

◆M◆E◆W◆P◆S◆N◆

2 teaspoons orange juice
2 teaspoons lemon juice
1 1/2 teaspoons milk-free, soy-free
   margarine, softened

1 cup confectioners sugar

In a small bowl, combine orange juice, lemon juice, and margarine. Beat with an electric mixer until smooth. Gradually add confectioners sugar; mix until smooth. Pour mixture over raisin bars.

Apple Blondies

◆M◆E◆P◆S◆N◆

4 1/2 tablespoons water, 4 1/2 tablespoons oil, 1 tablespoon baking
   powder; mixed together
1 3/4 cups sugar
1 cup oil
2 cups flour

1 teaspoon baking soda
1 teaspoon cinnamon
1/4 teaspoon salt
1 teaspoon vanilla extract
2 cups diced apples

Preheat oven to 375°. Grease a 9x12-inch pan and set aside. Mix water, oil, and baking powder mixture with sugar. Beat until thick and heavy. Add oil and beat well; set aside. In separate bowl, mix flour, baking soda, cinnamon, and salt. Beat slowly into liquid mixture. Fold in vanilla and apples. Pour batter into prepared pan. Bake for 40 minutes or until a wooden pick inserted in the center comes out clean. Cut when cool.

Caramel Crunch

◆M◆E◆P◆S◆N◆

5 cups Rice Chex cereal
5 cups Cheerios cereal
1/2 cup milk-free, soy-free margarine
1 cup light brown sugar

1/4 cup light corn syrup
1/2 teaspoon salt
1/4 teaspoon baking soda

Preheat oven to 200°. Pour the two cereals into a large roasting pan. Set aside. In a heavy saucepan, combine margarine, brown sugar, and corn syrup. Bring to a boil, stirring constantly. Boil 5 minutes. Remove from heat. Add salt and baking soda. Stir well. Pour syrup over cereal and mix well. Bake 30 minutes, stirring occasionally.

Suggestion: For variety, use 10 cups popped corn instead of cereal.

—Tracie Atkinson

M Milk-Free E Egg-Free W Wheat-Free

Poppy Seed Cookies

◆M◆E◆P◆S◆N◆

1 cup sugar
1/3 cup milk-free, soy-free margarine,
    softened
2 tablespoons light corn syrup
1 1/2 teaspoons vanilla extract
1 1/2 tablespoons water, 1 1/2 table-
    spoons oil, 1 teaspoon baking
    powder; mixed together

2 tablespoons water
2 1/4 cups flour
2 tablespoons poppy seeds
1 teaspoon baking soda

Preheat oven to 350°. Grease cookie sheets and set aside. In a large mixing bowl, cream sugar and margarine until fluffy. Add corn syrup; vanilla extract; and water, oil, and baking powder mixture; and the remaining 2 tablespoons water. Beat well and set aside. In another bowl, stir together flour, poppy seeds, and baking soda. Add to creamed mixture, blending well. Drop by rounded spoonfuls onto prepared sheets. Bake 12 minutes or until lightly browned. Let cool 1 minute. Move to wire racks to cool completely.

Halloween Cookie Pops

◆ M ◆ E ◆ P ◆ S ◆ N ◆

2/3 cup shortening
2/3 cup milk-free, soy-free margarine, softened
3/4 cup sugar
3/4 cup brown sugar, firmly packed
3 tablespoons water, 3 tablespoons oil, 2 teaspoons baking powder; mixed together

3 teaspoons vanilla extract
3 1/2 cups flour
2 teaspoons baking powder
1/2 teaspoon salt
3 teaspoons apple pie spice
popsicle sticks

Preheat oven to 375°. In large bowl, beat shortening, margarine, and sugars until creamy; beat in water, oil, and baking powder mixture and vanilla extract. Set aside. In another bowl, stir together flour, baking powder, salt, and apple pie spice; gradually add to margarine mixture, blending thoroughly. Chill dough 1 hour.

Have children cut out Halloween shapes from lightweight cardboard. Each pattern should be 5 to 6 inches wide.

Roll out dough onto lightly floured surface to 5/8-inch thickness. Place Halloween cutouts on dough and cut dough into shapes. Move to cookie sheets. Insert popsicle sticks about 1 to 2 inches deep into each cookie. Bake 10 minutes or until lightly browned. Transfer to cooling racks. Allow children to decorate with frosting when completely cooled.

Suggestion: Make Mickey Mouse-shaped cookie pops by rolling chilled dough into three balls, laying them next to each other, and flattening them with the bottom of a jar.

Tree Lights

◆M◆E◆P◆S◆N◆

1 1/2 cups flour	2 tablespoons oil
1/4 cup cornstarch	4 tablespoons water
1/4 teaspoon salt	1 1/2 teaspoons vanilla extract
3/4 cup confectioners sugar	red food coloring
5 tablespoons milk-free, soy-free	green food coloring
margarine, softened	1/2 cup confectioners sugar

Preheat oven to 350°. In a small bowl, stir together flour, corn-starch, and salt. Set aside. In a large bowl, using electric mixer, cream 3/4 cup confectioners sugar, margarine, and oil until smooth and light. Blend in water and vanilla extract, beating until smooth. Add dry ingredients and mix on low speed until just blended. Split dough in half. Add desired amount of red food col-oring to one half and green food coloring to the other half, blend-ing well.

Roll dough into 3/4-inch balls and place on ungreased cookie sheets. Bake 10 minutes or until lightly browned. While cookies are baking, sift 1/2 cup confectioners sugar into a shallow dish. When cookies are done, remove from oven and roll immediately in confectioners sugar. Cool on wire racks.

—Mariel Furlong

Christmas Tree

◆M◆E◆W◆P◆S◆N◆

3 tablespoons milk-free, soy-free	green food coloring
margarine	6 cups crisp rice cereal
10-ounce package milk-free, egg-free	decorations
marshmallows	

Generously grease a tree-shaped pan, equivalent to a 13x9x2-inch pan; set aside. Melt margarine in a large pot over low heat. Add marshmallows, stirring constantly until melted. Remove from heat. Stir in drops of green food coloring until desired color is achieved. Add cereal and stir well. Press mixture into prepared pan and refrigerate until chilled. Turn out onto greased waxed paper. Decorate with colored icing for ribbons or garland and confectioners sugar for snow. Use a variety of candies or dried fruits for ornaments.

—*Kathy Lundquist*

Frosting for Cookies

◆M◆ ◆E◆ ◆W◆ ◆P◆ ◆S◆ ◆N◆

1 3/4 cups confectioners sugar
1 1/2 tablespoons light corn syrup
1/2 teaspoon vanilla extract

1 drop lemon extract
1 1/2 tablespoons hot water

Sift confectioners sugar into a bowl. Add all remaining ingredients. Mix until smooth. If frosting is too thick, add a few more drops water.

Cakes, Pies, and Frostings

✦✦✦

The cake recipes in this section will taste good with a variety of frostings. Try changing frostings each time you make the cake.

These recipes can be made as cupcakes, sheet cakes, or layer cakes.

In place of icing, pour confectioners sugar over stencils that have been placed on top of the cake. Remove the stencil carefully.

Decorate cupcakes for holidays by adding colored frosting—orange frosting with chocolate cake for Halloween or coconut flakes and jelly beans for Easter.

Add cocoa or coconut flakes to pie crust recipes for a different taste.

To make a colorful, fun birthday cake, decorate the sides of a frosted cake with cut-out cookies, gumdrops, sprinkles, colored Life Savers, or striped candies.

Strawberry Cake

M E P S N

1/2 cup milk-free, soy-free
  margarine
2 cups sugar
4 1/2 cups cake flour
4 teaspoons baking powder
1/2 teaspoon salt

2 cups water
2 teaspoons vanilla extract
Strawberry Sauce (page 196)
Vanilla Frosting (page 164)
fresh strawberries

Preheat oven to 350°. Grease and flour two 8-inch round pans. Cream margarine and sugar until very light and fluffy. Sift together flour, baking powder, and salt; add alternately with water and vanilla to sugar mixture. Mix well with electric beater. Pour into two pans. Bake for 30 minutes or until cake tester comes out clean. Cool on wire rack.

Spread Strawberry Sauce on top of one layer. Put second layer on top. Frost the cake with Vanilla Frosting. Place fresh strawberries in a circle on the top.

Note: To make cupcakes, fill cupcake tins 2/3 full. Bake 30 minutes.

Carrot Cake

M E P S N

3/4 cup sugar
1 cup grated carrots
1 cup raisins
1 teaspoon cinnamon
1 teaspoon grated nutmeg
1/4 teaspoon ground cloves

1 1/2 cups water
3 tablespoons milk-free, soy-free
  margarine
2 cups flour
2 teaspoons baking soda
1/4 teaspoon salt

Preheat oven to 325°. Grease a 13x9-inch baking pan. In a medium saucepan, combine sugar, carrots, raisins, cinnamon, nutmeg, cloves, water, and margarine. Bring to a boil. Reduce heat, and simmer for 5 minutes.

Pour into a mixing bowl and let it cool. Add remaining ingredients; mix well. Pour into baking pan and bake for 40 minutes or until a cake tester comes out clean. Frost with white frosting, if desired.

Suggestion: Nuts may be added, if allowed.

Black Forest Cake

M E P S N

2 cups sugar	2 teaspoons baking soda
3/4 cup milk-free, soy-free margarine	3 tablespoons oil, 3 tablespoons water, 2 teaspoons baking powder; mixed together
1 1/2 cups boiling water	1 1/8 teaspoons vanilla extract
2 1/4 cups flour	cherry pie filling
1/2 cup cocoa	

Preheat oven to 350°. Grease and flour two round cake pans. Cream together the sugar and margarine. Add the water and beat together. Sift dry ingredients together and add to the mixture. Add oil, water, and baking powder mixture. Add vanilla and beat well. Pour the batter into pans. Bake 30 minutes.

When cooled, spread canned cherries on top of one layer, put the other layer on top and frost with Chocolate Frosting (recipe below). Top with cherry pie filling.

Chocolate Frosting

M E W P S N

2 1/2 cups confectioners sugar	1/4 cup water
1/2 cup unsweetened cocoa	1 teaspoon vanilla extract
1/2 cup milk-free, soy-free margarine	

Mix all ingredients except vanilla together in a saucepan. Bring to a full rolling boil and boil for one more minute. Remove from heat, add vanilla, and beat until creamy.

Ho Ho Sheet Cake

◆M◆ ◆E◆ ◆P◆ ◆N◆

3 cups flour

2 cups sugar

2 teaspoons baking soda

2/3 cup unsweetened cocoa powder

2 teaspoons vanilla extract

2 cups plus 2 teaspoons water

2 teaspoons vinegar

2/3 cup oil

Preheat oven to 350°. Grease 9x13-inch pan. Mix all ingredients thoroughly, and pour into pan. Bake for 45 minutes. Cool slightly. Put in refrigerator for 1/2 hour before putting first topping on.

First Topping

1 1/4 cups nondairy creamer

5 tablespoons flour

1 cup confectioners sugar

1/2 cup milk-free, soy-free margarine

1 cup shortening

In a saucepan, cook nondairy creamer and flour until thickened (pudding-like texture). Cool completely—it will be thick. In a bowl, cream confectioners sugar, margarine, and shortening. Add to cooled flour mixture. With an electric mixer, beat on high 5 minutes. Spread on cooled cake and return to refrigerator while preparing second topping.

Second Topping

1/2 cup milk-free, soy-free
    margarine

3 squares milk-free semi-sweet
    chocolate

1 1/2 cups confectioners sugar

1 1/2 tablespoons water, 1 1/2 table-
    spoons oil, 1 teaspoon baking
    powder; mixed together

1 teaspoon vanilla extract

1 teaspoon water

Melt together margarine and semi-sweet chocolate. Cool. In mixing bowl, mix remaining ingredients. Stir in chocolate and beat hard. Spread chocolate mix over first topping. (Make a design or stripes if you wish.) Store in refrigerator or cool place until ready to serve.

Suggestion: To make a layered cake, divide batter into two 8-inch round pans. Put white topping in middle and ice with chocolate topping. Put leftover white topping in a pastry bag and decorate the cake.
—*Robin Chadwell*

Pear Cake

4 cups chopped peeled pears (or drained canned pears)
2 cups sugar
3 cups flour
2 teaspoons baking soda
1/2 teaspoon salt
1/2 teaspoon ground nutmeg
1/2 teaspoon ground cinnamon

3 tablespoons water, 3 tablespoons oil, 2 teaspoons baking powder; mixed together
1 teaspoon vanilla extract
1 cup milk-free, soy-free margarine, softened
confectioners sugar

Combine pears and sugar; mix lightly. Let stand 1 hour, stirring frequently.

Preheat oven to 375°. Grease and flour a 10-inch Bundt pan or tube pan. Combine flour, baking soda, salt, and spices; set aside. Combine water, oil, and baking powder mixture with vanilla and margarine. Add to flour mixture; mix well. Stir in pear mixture.

Pour into prepared pan, spreading evenly to edges. Bake 1 hour and 15 minutes or until wooden pick inserted in center comes out clean. Cool in pan on wire rack 10 minutes. Loosen edges and remove from pan onto wire rack to cool completely. Dust lightly with confectioners sugar.

Notes: This cake freezes well.

One-quarter cup chopped raisins may be added while combining pears and sugar.

Wacky Chocolate Cake

◆M◆E◆P◆S◆N◆

1 1/2 cups flour
1 cup sugar
1/2 teaspoon salt
3 tablespoons unsweetened cocoa powder
1 teaspoon baking soda

1 teaspoon vanilla extract
1 tablespoon vinegar
5 tablespoons oil
1 cup cold water
confectioners sugar

Preheat oven to 350°. Sift dry ingredients into mixing bowl. Add vanilla, vinegar, oil, and water. Blend well; pour into ungreased 9-inch square pan. Bake for 25 to 30 minutes. When cool, frost or sprinkle confectioners sugar on top.

Suggestion: Omit cocoa powder, and add one mashed banana after adding water.

Spring Basket Cupcakes

◆M◆E◆P◆S◆N◆

White Birthday Cake (page 162)
Vanilla Frosting (page 164)
shredded coconut flakes

green food coloring
colored pipe cleaners

Preheat oven to 350°. Line muffin tin with paper liners. Use the recipe for the White Birthday Cake and fill cupcake cups half full. Bake for 25 minutes.

Frost with Vanilla Frosting. Put the coconut in a plastic bag, add a drop of green food coloring, and shake well. Sprinkle "grass" on top of cupcakes. Next, bend each pipe cleaner into an arc and place the ends into the top of each cupcake to make a basket handle.

Halloween Cupcakes

◆M◆ ◆E◆ ◆P◆ ◆S◆ ◆N◆

2 cups sugar
3/4 cup milk-free, soy-free
   margarine
1 1/2 cups boiling water
2 1/4 cups flour
1/2 cup cocoa

2 teaspoons baking soda
3 tablespoons oil, 3 tablespoons
   water, 2 teaspoons baking
   powder; mixed together
1 teaspoon vanilla extract
Orange Frosting (recipe below)

Preheat oven to 350°. Line muffin tin with paper liners. Cream together the sugar and margarine in a large mixing bowl. Add the boiling water and beat. Sift dry ingredients into this mixture and mix well. Add mixture of oil, water, and baking powder. Add the vanilla and beat for about 1 minute. Pour into muffin cups until 3/4 full. Bake 35 minutes. Decorate with Orange Frosting when cooled.

Orange Frosting

◆M◆ ◆E◆ ◆W◆ ◆P◆ ◆S◆ ◆N◆

2 tablespoons water
red and yellow food coloring
2 cups confectioners sugar

1 1/4 cups soft milk-free, soy-free
   margarine
1/8 teaspoon salt
1 teaspoon vanilla extract

Put enough drops of food coloring into the water to make desired orange color. Set aside. Cream half the sugar with margarine and salt in medium bowl. Blend in vanilla, 1 1/2 tablespoons colored water, and remaining sugar. Beat well, adding more colored water until desired spreading consistency is reached.

Barley-Carrot Cake

◆M◆ ◆E◆ ◆W◆ ◆P◆ ◆S◆ ◆N◆

1/4 cup molasses
1 1/2 cups oil
1 tablespoon vanilla extract
2 cups sugar
1 tablespoon cinnamon

1 teaspoon ginger
4 cups grated carrots
4 cups barley flour
2 teaspoons baking soda
2 tablespoons baking powder

Preheat oven to 350°. Grease a 9x13-inch pan. Blend well first 7 ingredients; set aside. Sift together dry ingredients. Combine with wet mixture. Pour into greased pan. Bake for 50 minutes. Cool.

White Birthday Cake

◆M◆ ◆E◆ ◆P◆ ◆S◆ ◆N◆

1/4 cup milk-free, soy-free margarine
3 cups sugar
4 1/2 cups cake flour

1 tablespoon baking powder
2 cups water
2 teaspoons vanilla extract

Preheat oven to 350°. Grease and flour two 8-inch round cake pans. Cream margarine and sugar until light and fluffy; set aside. Sift together cake flour and baking powder, and set aside. Mix together water and vanilla. Combine flour mixture, margarine mixture, and water/vanilla. Stir well. Pour into prepared pans. Bake 30 minutes or until cake tester comes out clean.

Cool 10 minutes in pan, then turn onto cake rack. Frost when completely cooled with lemon or chocolate frosting. If preferred, drizzle Raspberry Sauce (page 196) on top instead of frosting.

Orange Cupcakes

◆M◆E◆W◆P◆S◆N◆

1/4 cup shortening
1/2 cup sugar
1 cup plus 2 tablespoons rice flour
1/4 teaspoon salt
1/4 teaspoon cinnamon

1/4 teaspoon ginger
1/4 teaspoon nutmeg
1 1/4 teaspoons baking powder
1/2 cup orange juice

Preheat oven to 375°. Line muffin tin with paper liners. Soften shortening, and add sugar; cream until light and fluffy. Mix dry ingredients together. Add dry ingredients and orange juice to shortening-sugar mixture. Beat on low speed for 30 seconds. Fill muffin cups 2/3 full. Bake for 20 to 30 minutes.

Note: These cupcakes hold together better if you let them cool a few hours or overnight.

—Nancy Sanker

Fudge Upside-Down Cake

◆M◆E◆P◆S◆N◆

3/4 cup granulated sugar
1 tablespoon milk-free, soy-free
   margarine
1/2 cup water
1 cup flour

1/4 teaspoon salt
1 teaspoon baking powder
1 1/2 tablespoons unsweetened cocoa
   powder

Preheat oven to 350°. Grease a 9-inch square pan. Cream together sugar and margarine. Add water and stir. Sift together flour, salt, baking powder, and cocoa and add to sugar mixture. Stir well and pour into pan.

Topping

1/2 cup granulated sugar
1/2 cup brown sugar

1/4 cup unsweetened cocoa powder
1 1/4 cups boiling water

Mix sugars and cocoa well. Spread onto mixture in pan. Top with boiling water poured evenly. Bake for 30 minutes. Let cool in pan.

Lemon Frosting

◆◆◆◆◆◆

2 cups confectioners sugar
1 1/4 cups milk-free, soy-free margarine,
   softened

1/8 teaspoon salt
1 teaspoon lemon extract
2 tablespoons water

Cream half the sugar with margarine and salt. Blend in lemon extract, 1 1/2 tablespoons water, and remaining sugar. Beat well, adding more water until desired spreading consistency is reached.

Cinnamon-Chocolate Frosting

◆◆◆◆◆◆

1/3 cup milk-free, soy-free margarine,
   softened
1 1/2 pounds confectioners sugar
1/3 cup unsweetened cocoa powder

1 teaspoon ground cinnamon
3/4 teaspoon vanilla extract
1/3 cup water

Combine all ingredients in a medium bowl. Beat together until smooth. Add more water if needed to reach desired consistency.

Vanilla Frosting

◆◆◆◆◆◆

2/3 cup solid vegetable shortening
1-pound box confectioners sugar

3 tablespoons water
1 teaspoon vanilla extract

Cream shortening and sugar until well blended. Add water. Beat until smooth. Chill at least one hour. Beat again and add vanilla.

Note: This frosting works well for making flowers or other decorations. It can be made with lemon or orange extract instead of vanilla.

Glazed Peach Pie

◆M◆ ◆E◆ ◆W◆ ◆P◆ ◆S◆ ◆N◆

4 cups sliced, peeled fresh peaches
3/4 cup sugar
3-ounce package orange gelatin
1/8 teaspoon salt

1 cup hot water
1/2 cup cold water
4 teaspoons lemon juice
1 baked 9-inch pie shell*

Combine peaches and sugar; let stand for 10 minutes. Dissolve gelatin and salt in 1 cup hot water; add cold water and lemon juice. Add peaches and chill until slightly thickened. Turn into cooled pie shell, arranging the peaches evenly. Chill before serving.

*Rice Pie Crust (below) works well.

Colorful Coconut Icing

◆M◆ ◆E◆ ◆W◆ ◆P◆ ◆S◆ ◆N◆

3/4 cup unsweetened shredded coconut
food coloring

1 1/2 cups honey
3/4 cup water

Put coconut into a plastic bag, and add food coloring; shake well. Add more food coloring until desired color is reached. Set aside. Mix honey and water to get a thin consistency. Drizzle over cake; top with colored coconut.

Rice Pie Crust

◆M◆ ◆E◆ ◆W◆ ◆P◆ ◆S◆ ◆N◆

4 1/2 cups crisp rice cereal, crushed
3 tablespoons brown sugar

1/3 cup milk-free, soy-free
    margarine

Preheat oven to 300°. Combine cereal and brown sugar. Mix well. Melt margarine and pour over mixture; mix until well coated. Pack firmly into bottom and sides of an 8-inch or 9-inch pie pan. Bake for 10 to 12 minutes.

Rye Pie Crust

◆◆◆◆◆◆

1 cup rye flour
1/2 teaspoon salt

1/3 cup shortening
3 tablespoons cold water

Preheat the oven to 450°. Mix the flour and salt. Using a fork, cut in the shortening until mixture is the size of peas. Sprinkle with water, one tablespoon at a time. Blend lightly with a fork until all the flour is moistened. Roll out on a floured board. Carefully lift the pastry into the pie shell. Prick the pastry several times on the bottom and sides with a fork. Bake for 10 to 12 minutes.

Note: This recipe is good for tarts.

Cornflake Crumb Crust

◆◆◆◆◆◆

1 cup prepackaged cornflake crumbs
2 tablespoons sugar

1/3 cup milk-free, soy-free
margarine, softened

Preheat oven to 375°. Combine ingredients; mix thoroughly. Press evenly into a 9-inch pie pan. Bake 5 minutes. Chill.

—Nancy Sanker

◆ Milk-Free ◆ Egg-Free ◆ Wheat-Free

Glazed Strawberry Pie

♦Ⓜ Ⓔ Ⓦ Ⓟ Ⓢ Ⓝ♦

1 quart strawberries

1 cup sugar

1 cup water

2 1/2 tablespoons cornstarch

1/8 teaspoon salt

9-inch pie shell*

confectioners sugar

In a saucepan, combine 1 cup strawberries with 3/4 cup sugar and 1 cup water. Cook for 5 minutes over high heat. Remove from heat and mash with a fork. Add cornstarch, remaining 1/4 cup sugar and salt; stir well. Return to heat. Cook until thickened, stirring continuously. Place remaining strawberries in the pie shell; pour in strawberry glaze. Chill. Sprinkle confectioners sugar on top just before serving, if desired.

*Rice Pie Crust (page 165) works well.

Morning Glory Cake

♦Ⓜ Ⓔ Ⓟ Ⓢ Ⓝ♦

1 1/3 cups flour

3/4 teaspoon baking soda

1/4 teaspoon salt

2/3 cup sugar

3/4 teaspoon ground ginger

3/4 cup unsweetened applesauce

1/4 cup oil

3 tablespoons molasses

1 1/2 tablespoons water, 1 1/2 tablespoons oil, 1 teaspoon baking
powder; mixed together

1 tablespoon sugar

1/4 teaspoon ground allspice

Preheat oven to 350°. Grease an 8-inch square baking pan. In a large bowl, combine flour, baking soda, salt, 2/3 cup sugar, and ginger; stir well. Set aside. In another bowl, combine applesauce; oil; molasses; and water, oil, and baking powder mixture. Add to dry ingredients. Stir just until dry ingredients are moistened.

Spoon batter into prepared pan. Combine remaining tablespoon of sugar and allspice; sprinkle over batter. Bake 35 minutes or until a cake tester inserted in center comes out clean. Cool 10 minutes in pan on a wire rack.

Triple-Layer Chocolate Coconut Cake

◆M◆E◆P◆S◆N

1 cup milk-free, soy-free margarine, softened
1 3/4 cups sugar
1 tablespoon vanilla extract
4 1/2 tablespoons water, 4 1/2 tablespoons oil, 1 tablespoon baking powder; mixed together

2 1/4 cups cake flour
1 cup unsweetened cocoa powder
1 1/2 teaspoons baking powder
1 teaspoon baking soda
1/4 teaspoon salt
1 3/4 cups water
Vanilla Coconut Frosting (below)

Preheat oven to 350°. Grease three 9-inch round baking pans. In a large bowl, beat the margarine, sugar, and vanilla extract until light and fluffy. Add the water, oil, and baking powder mixture and beat well. Set aside. In a medium bowl, combine the flour, cocoa, baking powder, baking soda, and salt. Stir well. Combine flour mixture with liquid mixture. Stir until well blended. Add water and stir until well blended. Divide the batter into the prepared pans.

Bake 25 to 30 minutes, or until a cake tester inserted in center comes out clean. Place pans on wire racks and let stand 10 minutes. Remove cake layers from pans and let cool completely. Frost layers with Vanilla Coconut Frosting. Stack layers to make a triple-layer cake.

Vanilla Coconut Frosting

◆M◆E◆W◆P◆S◆N

3 cups confectioners sugar
1/3 cup water
2 teaspoons light corn syrup

1 teaspoon vanilla extract
1/4 teaspoon cream of tartar
1/2 cup flaked coconut

Put all ingredients except coconut in a bowl and mix well. Frost layers of cake. Top each layer with flaked coconut.

Moist Spice Cake

◆M◆E◆P◆S◆N◆

2 cups flour
3/4 cup sugar
3/4 cup apple juice
3 tablespoons water, 3 tablespoons oil,
   2 teaspoons baking powder;
   mixed together
1/2 cup brown sugar, firmly packed
1/2 cup shortening

2 1/2 teaspoons baking powder
1/2 teaspoon ground cloves
1/2 teaspoon nutmeg
1 teaspoon salt
1 teaspoon cinnamon
1 teaspoon allspice
1 teaspoon vanilla extract
Creamy Frosting (recipe below)

Preheat oven to 350°. Grease and flour two 8-inch round cake pans. Pour all ingredients into a large bowl. Beat until ingredients are well blended. Pour batter into prepared cake pans. Bake 25 to 30 minutes or until a cake tester inserted in center comes out clean. Cool layers 10 minutes in pans on wire racks; remove from pans and cool completely on wire racks before frosting with Creamy Frosting.

Creamy Frosting

◆M◆E◆W◆P◆S◆N◆

4 cups confectioners sugar
3 tablespoons water

3 tablespoons milk-free, soy-free
   margarine, melted
1 tablespoon vanilla extract

In a large bowl, beat all ingredients. Add more water, if necessary, to reach good spreading consistency.

Apple Upside-Down Cake

◆M◆E◆P◆S◆N

1 large apple, peeled and cored
3 tablespoons brown sugar
1/4 cup white sugar
1/4 cup oil
1 1/2 tablespoons water, 1 1/2 tablespoons oil, 1 teaspoon baking
powder; mixed together
1/2 cup dark molasses

1 1/3 cups flour
1 teaspoon ground ginger
3/4 teaspoon baking powder
1/2 teaspoon salt
1/2 teaspoon ground cinnamon
1/4 teaspoon ground cloves
1/2 cup hot water

Preheat oven to 350°. Grease a 10-inch round cake pan. Slice apple crosswise into 1/4-inch thick rings. Place apple rings and brown sugar in a bowl; toss gently. Let stand 5 minutes. Arrange apples in a single layer in prepared cake pan. Bake 15 minutes.

In a large mixing bowl, combine white sugar; oil; and water, oil, and baking powder mixture; beat at medium speed. Add molasses. Beat until well blended. Set aside.

Combine flour, ginger, baking powder, salt, cinnamon, and cloves. Add to sugar mixture. Add hot water and mix well. Spoon batter over apple rings. Bake 30 minutes or until a cake tester inserted in center comes out clean. Cool in pan 10 minutes.

Suggestion: Sprinkle confectioners sugar on top when cool.

Chocolate Applesauce Sheet Cake

◆M◆E◆P◆S◆N

2 cups flour
1 cup white sugar
1/4 cup brown sugar, firmly packed
1/4 cup unsweetened cocoa powder
2 teaspoons baking soda

2 teaspoons cinnamon
1/4 teaspoon ground cloves
1 1/2 cups applesauce
1/4 cup oil
2 teaspoons vanilla extract

Preheat oven to 350°. Grease a 13 x 9-inch pan. Combine flour, both sugars, cocoa, baking soda, cinnamon, and cloves. Stir well. Add applesauce, oil, and vanilla extract. Beat until well blended.

Pour into prepared pan. Bake 30 minutes or until a cake tester inserted in center comes out clean.

Suggestions: This recipe works well for cupcakes, too. Top with your favorite frosting. To decorate for holidays, make stencils of bunnies, pumpkins, and such. Place on top of cake and sprinkle with confectioners sugar.

Coconut-Banana Coffee Cake

◆ M ◆ E ◆ P ◆ S ◆ N

1 3/4 cups flour
1/2 teaspoon baking soda
1/4 teaspoon salt
1 1/4 teaspoons cream of tartar
1/3 cup sugar
1 large banana, mashed
1/4 cup milk-free, soy-free margarine, melted

1/4 cup water
1 1/2 tablespoons water, 1 1/2 tablespoons oil, 1 teaspoon baking powder; mixed together
1 teaspoon vanilla extract
3 tablespoons coconut flakes
2 teaspoons ground cinnamon

Preheat oven to 350°. Grease an 8-inch square pan. Set aside. In a mixing bowl, combine flour, baking soda, salt, cream of tartar, and sugar. Mix well. Add banana; margarine; water; water, oil, and baking powder mixture; and vanilla extract. Stir until all ingredients are well blended. Pour batter into prepared pan. In a separate bowl, combine coconut and cinnamon. Sprinkle coconut and cinnamon mixture on batter. Bake 25 minutes or until a cake tester inserted in center comes out clean. Remove from oven and cool on wire rack. Remove from pan and let cool completely on wire rack before serving.

Banana Upside-Down Cake

◆M◆E◆P◆S◆N◆

3 tablespoons milk-free, soy-free
  margarine
1/2 cup brown sugar, firmly packed
4 firm bananas
1 1/2 tablespoons water, 1 1/2 tablespoons oil, 1 teaspoon baking
  powder; mixed together
1/2 cup sugar
3 tablespoons oil

2 tablespoons water
1 teaspoon vanilla extract
1/2 teaspoon grated orange peel
1 cup flour
1 teaspoon baking powder
1/2 teaspoon ground cinnamon
1/4 teaspoon baking soda
1/8 teaspoon salt

Preheat oven to 350°. Melt margarine in a 9-inch square cake pan. Stir in brown sugar. Peel and slice 3 bananas. Arrange slices in single layer in brown sugar mixture; set aside. Cut remaining banana into chunks. Place banana chunks; water, oil, and baking powder mixture; sugar; oil; water; vanilla extract; and orange peel in food processor or blender. Process until smooth. Set aside.

In large bowl, combine flour, baking powder, cinnamon, baking soda, and salt. Combine banana mixture with flour mixture. Stir until well mixed. Pour batter over bananas in pan. Bake 30 minutes or until a cake tester inserted in center comes out clean. Cool in pan 5 minutes. Invert onto serving plate.

Suggestion: This makes an interesting breakfast!

Fruit Crisp

◆M◆E◆W◆P◆S◆N◆

16-ounce can sliced peaches
1/4 cup cornstarch
2 tablespoons brown sugar

2 tablespoons milk-free, soy-free
  margarine
1/4 cup quick oats

Preheat oven to 450°. Grease a 1-quart casserole dish. Drain peaches and place in casserole dish. Set aside. Blend together cornstarch, brown sugar, and margarine. Mix in oats. (Mixture will be lumpy.) Pour over peaches. Bake 20 minutes or until lightly browned.

Pear Pie

5 cups sliced canned pears, drained
1/2 cup quick-cooking tapioca
2 tablespoons lemon juice

2 tablespoons pear juice from canned
   pears
2 (9-inch) pie crusts

Preheat oven to 350°. In a large bowl, combine pears and tapioca. Mix well. Add lemon juice and pear juice. Blend thoroughly. Place one pie crust in pie pan; add pear mixture. Top with remaining pie crust. Bake 50 minutes or until pie crust is light golden brown.

Notes: This recipe can also be made with a rice flour or other non-wheat-flour pie crust. If using fresh pears, replace pear juice with water and add 1/4 cup sugar.

Powdered Sugar Doughnuts

1 1/2 cups flour
1/2 cup sugar
1 1/2 teaspoons baking powder
1 teaspoon ground cinnamon
1/2 teaspoon ground nutmeg
1/4 teaspoon salt
1/2 cup water

1/4 cup milk-free, soy-free
   margarine, melted
1 1/2 tablespoons oil, 1 1/2 tablespoons water, 1 teaspoon baking
   powder; mixed together
1/2 teaspoon vanilla extract
confectioners sugar

Preheat oven to 400°. Grease miniature Bundt pans. In large mixing bowl, combine flour, sugar, baking powder, cinnamon, nutmeg, and salt. Add water; margarine; oil, water, and baking powder mixture; and vanilla extract. Blend thoroughly. Pour batter into prepared pans. Cook 12 minutes or until a cake tester inserted in center comes out clean. Remove from oven. Remove doughnuts from pan and place on wire rack to cool. Top generously with confectioners sugar.

Note: To make doughnut holes, use miniature muffin tins instead of miniature Bundt pans and cook 9 to 10 minutes.

Pumpkin Frosting

◆M◆ ◆E◆ ◆W◆ ◆P◆ ◆S◆ ◆N◆

5 cups confectioners sugar
1/2 cup milk-free, soy-free margarine,
    softened
2 teaspoons vanilla extract

1/4 cup water
orange food coloring
green food coloring

Beat all ingredients except food coloring together on medium speed until smooth and of spreading consistency. If necessary, stir in additional water, 1 teaspoon at a time. Divide frosting in half. Add different color food coloring to each half. Use orange frosting for pumpkins and green frosting for stems.

Fudge Frosting

◆M◆ ◆E◆ ◆W◆ ◆P◆ ◆S◆ ◆N◆

1/3 cup milk-free, soy-free margarine,
    softened
1/3 cup unsweetened cocoa powder

1 teaspoon vanilla extract
2 cups confectioners sugar, divided
2 tablespoons water

Mix together margarine and cocoa. Gradually stir in vanilla extract and half the confectioners sugar. Add water. Add the remaining sugar, and stir until smooth. Add more water if frosting is too thick.

—Marguerite Furlong

Banana Frosting

◆M◆ ◆E◆ ◆W◆ ◆P◆ ◆S◆ ◆N◆

2 tablespoons shortening
1 mashed banana

1 teaspoon water
2 cups confectioners sugar

Combine shortening with mashed banana and water in medium bowl. Beat at medium speed until well blended. Add confectioners sugar. Beat until well blended.

Coconut-Apple Pie

M E P S N

2 (9-inch) unbaked pie crusts
3/4 cup sugar
1 tablespoon cornstarch
1 teaspoon cinnamon
1/4 teaspoon nutmeg

1/2 cup flaked coconut
5 cups baking apples, peeled and
   thinly sliced
1 tablespoon sugar

Preheat oven to 400°. Place one pie crust in a pie pan; set aside. In a bowl, mix 3/4 cup sugar, cornstarch, cinnamon, nutmeg, and coconut. Add apples and mix well. Spoon mixture into crust. Place remaining pie crust over apple mixture. Crimp edges and sprinkle remaining sugar on top of pie crust. Bake 45 to 50 minutes or until crust is golden brown.

Valentine Cupcakes

M E P S N

1 1/2 cups flour
1 cup sugar
1 teaspoon baking powder
1 teaspoon baking soda
1/2 teaspoon salt

5 tablespoons milk-free, soy-free
   margarine, melted
1 teaspoon vanilla extract
1 cup cold water
Valentine Frosting (recipe below)

Preheat oven to 350°. Line muffin tin with paper liners. In a large bowl mix all ingredients except frosting together and blend well. Pour the mixture into muffin tins. Bake 20 to 25 minutes or until a cake tester inserted in the center comes out clean. Frost when completely cooled.

Valentine Frosting

M E W S P N

1 cup confectioners sugar
2 tablespoons milk-free, soy-free
   margarine, softened

1 teaspoon water
red food coloring

In small bowl, mix confectioners sugar, margarine, water, and enough drops of red food coloring to achieve desired color. Add more water if necessary to make frosting spreadable.

Banana Cake

vegetable cooking spray
2 cups flour
3/4 cup brown sugar, firmly packed
1 teaspoon baking powder
1 teaspoon baking soda
1/2 teaspoon salt
1 3/4 cups ripe banana, mashed
   (about 4 medium bananas)
1/2 cup oil

Preheat oven to 350°. Coat Bundt pan with vegetable cooking spray and set aside. In a large bowl, combine flour, brown sugar, baking powder, baking soda, and salt. Stir well. Set aside. In another bowl, combine banana and oil. Stir well. Add banana and oil mixture to dry ingredients, stirring just until moistened. Spoon batter into Bundt pan.

Bake 40 to 50 minutes or until a cake tester inserted in center comes out clean. Cool in pan 10 minutes, then remove and cool completely on wire rack.

Suggestion: This cake can be served for breakfast or topped with a chocolate glaze and served at a party.

Chocolate Fudge Cake

1 cup flour
1/2 cup sugar
4 tablespoons unsweetened cocoa
   powder, divided
1 1/2 teaspoons baking powder
1/4 teaspoon salt
1/2 cup water
1 1/2 tablespoons oil
1 1/2 teaspoons vanilla extract
1/3 cup sugar
1/8 teaspoon salt
1 1/2 cups boiling water
sliced kiwis, strawberries, or
   raspberries

Preheat oven to 350°. Grease a 9-inch square baking pan. In a medium bowl, combine flour, sugar, 2 tablespoons cocoa, baking powder, and salt and stir well. Set aside. In another bowl, combine water, oil, and vanilla extract. Add to dry ingredients and stir well. Spoon batter into pan.

In a small bowl, mix together sugar, remaining cocoa, and salt. Sprinkle evenly over batter. Pour boiling water over batter. Do not stir. Bake 30 minutes or until cake springs back when lightly touched in center. Put plate on top and invert pan. Top cake with fruit.

Snacking Cake

Ⓜ Ⓔ Ⓟ Ⓢ Ⓝ

1 1/2 cups flour	1/2 cup oil
1 teaspoon baking soda	1/2 cup brown sugar, firmly packed
1 teaspoon cinnamon	1/2 cup white sugar
1/2 teaspoon nutmeg	1 1/2 cups finely grated carrots
1/2 teaspoon salt	(about 4 large)
3 tablespoons oil, 3 tablespoons water, 2 teaspoons baking powder; mixed together	8-ounce can crushed pineapple packed in juice, undrained

Preheat oven to 350°. Grease a 9-inch square or 7x11-inch pan. In a large bowl, mix together flour, baking soda, cinnamon, nutmeg, and salt. Set aside. In another bowl, combine oil, water, and baking powder mixture with oil. Add sugars, and stir well. Set aside. In a third bowl, combine the carrots and pineapple with its juice. Set aside.

Stir the sugar mixture into the dry ingredients. Stir in the carrot-pineapple mixture. Spoon batter into the prepared pan. Bake 30 to 40 minutes or until a cake tester inserted in the center comes out clean.

Suggestion: This cake is delicious! Top with confectioners sugar poured over a doily to dress it up for dessert or a party.

White Cake

◆M◆◆E◆◆P◆◆N◆◆S◆

1/3 cup shortening or scant 1/3 cup oil
3/4 cup sugar
1/2 teaspoon salt
3 tablespoons plus 1/4 teaspoon flour
3 tablespoons water
2 1/4 teaspoons oil

2 teaspoons lemon juice
1 1/2 cups plus 2 tablespoons flour
3/4 cup water
3 1/2 teaspoons baking powder
Lemon Frosting (recipe below)

Preheat oven to 375°. Grease and flour a 9-inch square baking pan and set aside. In a large bowl, cream together shortening, sugar, and salt. Set aside. In a small bowl, combine 3 tablespoons plus 1/4 teaspoon flour, 3 tablespoons water, and oil. Stir well; combine with sugar mixture. Beat well. Stir in lemon juice. Add remaining flour and water; beat 1 to 2 minutes. Add baking powder; beat well but quickly. Pour mixture into prepared pan. Bake 30 minutes or until a cake tester inserted in center comes out clean.

Lemon Frosting

◆M◆◆E◆◆W◆◆P◆◆S◆◆N◆

1 1/2 cups confectioners sugar
1 tablespoon oil

1 1/4 teaspoons lemon juice
5 teaspoons water

In a large bowl, combine ingredients for lemon frosting. Mix well. Add more water if necessary. Frost cake when cooled.

French Apple Tart

◆M◆E◆P◆S◆N◆

Crust

1/2 cup shortening
1/2 cup plus 2 tablespoons sugar
2 teaspoons baking powder

2 1/4 cups flour
1 tablespoon water
1 tablespoon vinegar

Filling

3 large apples, peeled and sliced

10-ounce jar strawberry jam or jelly

Preheat oven to 375°. Combine crust ingredients in bowl. Knead by hand until all ingredients are combined. Flatten inside a spring-form pan or pie tin. Top with apples arranged in a circle. Warm jam or jelly in microwave for approximately one minute or until pourable. Pour over apples. Bake 1 hour.

—*Terry Hess*

Swirl Cake

◆M◆E◆P◆S◆N◆

1 3/4 cups sugar
2/3 cup milk-free, soy-free margarine, softened
1/4 cup oil, 1/4 cup water, 1 table-spoon baking powder; mixed together
2 teaspoons vanilla extract
3 cups cake flour

2 1/2 teaspoons baking powder
1/2 teaspoon salt
1 2/3 cups water
1/4 cup sugar
1/2 cup unsweetened cocoa powder
1/4 cup water
Smooth Chocolate Frosting (recipe page 181)

Preheat the oven to 350°. Grease and flour two 9-inch baking pans. Set aside. In a large bowl, using an electric mixer, beat 1 3/4 cups sugar and the margarine until light and fluffy. Add the oil, water, and baking powder mixture. Beat in the vanilla extract. Set aside.

In a small bowl, combine flour, baking powder, and salt. Add 1 2/3 cups water. Add to margarine mixture. Stir until well combined. Set aside. In a small bowl, combine the remaining 1/4 cup sugar and the cocoa. Gradually stir in 1/4 cup water until smooth. Fold 1 1/2 cups batter into the cocoa mixture until smooth. Divide the remaining batter between the prepared pans. Drop the cocoa batter by tablespoonfuls into the prepared pans. Swirl the batter with a fork. Bake 35 to 40 minutes or until a cake tester inserted in center comes out clean. Frost when completely cooled.

Heavenly Chocolate Cupcakes

◆M◆E◆P◆S◆N◆

2 cups sugar	2 teaspoons baking soda
1 cup unsweetened cocoa powder	1 teaspoon baking powder
1 cup milk-free, soy-free margarine	1/2 teaspoon salt
2 cups water	1 teaspoon vanilla extract
3 tablespoons oil, 3 tablespoons water, 2 teaspoons baking powder; mixed together	4 cups flour
	Minty Frosting (recipe below)

Preheat oven to 400°. Line muffin tin with paper liners. Set aside. In large bowl, combine everything but flour. Beat until well mixed. Stir in flour and mix well. Fill muffin tins 2/3 full. Bake 18 minutes or until cake tester inserted in middle comes out clean. Remove to wire rack to cool before frosting.

Minty Frosting

◆M◆E◆W◆P◆S◆N◆

4 cups confectioners sugar	2 tablespoons water
1 cup milk-free, soy-free margarine, softened	2 teaspoons vanilla extract
	1/2 teaspoon mint extract
1 teaspoon salt	

In small bowl, combine all ingredients. Beat until light and fluffy.

Smooth Chocolate Frosting

◆M◆E◆W◆P◆S◆N◆

2 cups confectioners sugar
1/4 cup milk-free, soy-free margarine, melted

2 tablespoons water
2 teaspoons unsweetened cocoa powder

In a small bowl, combine all ingredients. Using an electric mixer, mix until smooth.

Decadent Chocolate Frosting

◆M◆E◆W◆P◆S◆N◆

1/2 cup milk-free, soy-free margarine, softened
1/2 cup unsweetened cocoa powder

1/3 cup water
1 teaspoon vanilla extract
3 cups confectioners sugar

In a small bowl, combine margarine, cocoa powder, water, and vanilla extract. Beat smooth with electric mixer. Add confectioners sugar and beat until spreadable consistency.

Note: This frosting can be used on vanilla cookies, brownies, or any of your favorite treats.

Creamy Vanilla Frosting

◆M◆E◆W◆P◆S◆N◆

1 1/2 cups milk-free, soy-free margarine, softened
4 cups confectioners sugar

2 tablespoons water
1 teaspoon vanilla extract
food coloring (optional)

Beat margarine at medium speed with an electric mixer until soft and creamy. Gradually add sugar. Beat until light and fluffy. Add water, vanilla extract, and, if desired, food coloring. Beat until frosting reaches proper consistency.

Applesauce Brownies

◆M◆E◆P◆S◆N◆

1 cup firmly packed brown sugar
1/2 cup milk-free, soy-free margarine,
   softened
3 tablespoons water, 3 tablespoons oil,
   2 teaspoons baking powder; mixed
   together
1 cup applesauce

1 teaspoon vanilla extract
1 cup flour
1/4 cup unsweetened cocoa powder
1 teaspoon ground cinnamon
1/2 teaspoon baking powder
1/2 teaspoon baking soda
1/4 teaspoon salt

Preheat oven to 350°. Grease 9-inch square pan. Set aside. In a large bowl, combine sugar and margarine with the water, oil, and baking powder mixture. Stir well. Add applesauce and vanilla extract; blend well. Add flour, cocoa powder, cinnamon, baking powder, baking soda, and salt. Mix well. Pour into prepared pan. Bake 35 minutes or until wooden toothpick inserted in center comes out clean. Cool completely in pan on wire rack.

Three-Layer Chocolate Cake

◆M◆E◆P◆S◆N◆

1 1/3 cups cake flour
1 teaspoon baking soda
1/4 teaspoon salt
1/2 cup milk-free, soy-free margarine,
   softened
1 1/3 cups sugar

3 tablespoons water, 3 tablespoons
   oil, 2 teaspoons baking powder;
   mixed together
1/2 cup plus 1 tablespoon
   unsweetened cocoa powder
2/3 cup water
1 teaspoon vanilla extract

Preheat oven to 350°. Grease three 8-inch round cake pans. Set aside. In a small bowl, sift together flour, baking soda, and salt. Set aside. In a large bowl, beat margarine and sugar until creamy. Add all remaining ingredients. Blend well. Add flour mixture. Mix thoroughly. Pour evenly into prepared pans. Bake 18 to 20 minutes. Cool in pans on wire racks 10 minutes. Remove from pans and cool completely. Frost with Creamy Cocoa Frosting (page 185).

Note: Layers will only be 1/4 inch to 1/2 inch high.

Chocolate Pound Cake

◆E◆P◆S◆N◆

3/4 cup milk-free, soy-free margarine, softened
1 1/2 cups sugar
4 1/2 tablespoons water, 4 1/2 tablespoons oil, 1 tablespoon baking powder; mixed together
1 1/2 cups water

1 teaspoon baking soda
3 1/2 cups flour
3/4 cup unsweetened cocoa powder
1 teaspoon baking powder
1/4 teaspoon salt
2 teaspoons vanilla extract
1 teaspoon confectioners sugar

Preheat oven to 350°. Grease Bundt pan. Set aside. In a large mixing bowl, cream together margarine and sugar. Add water, oil, and baking powder mixture. Mix well. Set aside. In a separate bowl, combine water and baking soda. Stir. Set aside. In a medium bowl, sift together flour, cocoa, baking powder, and salt. Add dry ingredients to creamed mixture. Add water and baking soda mixture. Stir in vanilla extract. Blend well. Pour mixture into Bundt pan. Bake 45 minutes or until a wooden pick inserted in center comes out clean. Cool in pan 10 minutes. Remove from pan and cool completely on wire rack. Top cake with confectioners sugar.

Chocolate Wacky Cupcakes

◆E◆W◆P◆S◆N◆

2 cups rice flour
1 cup sugar
1/2 teaspoon salt
3 tablespoons unsweetened cocoa powder
1 teaspoon baking soda

1 teaspoon vanilla extract
1 tablespoon vinegar
5 tablespoons oil
1 cup cold water

Preheat oven to 350°. Line muffin pan with paper liners. Set aside. In a large mixing bowl, stir together flour, sugar, salt, cocoa, and baking soda. Add vanilla extract, vinegar, oil, and water. Mix thoroughly. Pour batter into muffin cups and bake 25 to 30 minutes or until done.

Gingerbread Cake

ⓂⒺⓅⓈⓃ

2 1/2 cups flour
2 teaspoons baking soda
1/2 teaspoon salt
1 tablespoon ground ginger
1/2 cup shortening
1/4 cup brown sugar, firmly packed

3 tablespoons water, 3 tablespoons
   oil, 2 teaspoons baking powder;
   mixed together
1 cup molasses
1 cup boiling water

Preheat oven to 375°. Grease and flour an 8-inch square pan. Set aside. In a medium bowl, stir together flour, baking soda, salt, and ginger. Set aside. In a large bowl, cream shortening and brown sugar until light and fluffy. Beat in water, oil, and baking powder mixture. Add molasses. Blend well. Stir in water. Quickly add flour mixture and stir until batter is smooth. Spread batter evenly into prepared pan. Bake 35 to 40 minutes or until a cake tester inserted in center comes out clean. May be served warm or cold.

Chocolate Date Cake

ⓂⒺⓅⓈⓃ

1 cup hot water
2/3 cup chopped dates
1 2/3 cups flour
1 cup packed brown sugar
1/4 cup unsweetened cocoa powder
1 teaspoon baking soda

1/2 teaspoon salt
1/4 cup oil
1 teaspoon cider vinegar
1/2 teaspoon vanilla extract
3 tablespoons packed brown sugar

Preheat oven to 350°. In small bowl, pour hot water over dates. Allow to stand 5 minutes. Drain dates and reserve the water. Set aside. In ungreased 8-inch square baking dish, mix flour, 1 cup brown sugar, cocoa, baking soda, and salt. Stir in dates. Add water to reserved date water to measure 1 cup. Add water, oil, vinegar, and vanilla extract to flour mixture. Mix well. Sprinkle with 3 table-spoons brown sugar. Bake 40 minutes or until wooden pick inserted in center comes out clean.

Apple-Butter Spice Cake

◆M◆E◆P◆S◆N

1 tablespoon milk-free, soy-free
  margarine, melted
1 cup apple butter
3/4 cup brown sugar, firmly packed
3 tablespoons oil
1/2 cup raisins
1/2 cup water
1 1/2 tablespoons water, 1 1/2 tablespoons oil, 1 teaspoon baking
  powder; mixed together

2 teaspoons vanilla extract
2 cups plus 2 tablespoons flour
2 teaspoons baking soda
2 teaspoons ground cinnamon
2 teaspoons ground ginger
1 teaspoon ground allspice
1/4 teaspoon salt

Preheat oven to 350°. Lightly grease an 8-inch square baking pan and set aside. In a mixing bowl, combine margarine, apple butter, brown sugar, and oil, and stir until smooth. Add raisins; water; and water, oil, and baking powder mixture. Stir well. Add vanilla extract and stir again. Add all remaining ingredients. Beat until combined. Pour batter into prepared pan. Bake 35 minutes, or until a wooden pick inserted in the center comes out clean. Allow to cool before serving.

Creamy Cocoa Frosting

◆M◆E◆W◆P◆S◆N

1 1/2 cups milk-free, soy-free
  margarine, softened
4 cups confectioners sugar, divided

1/4 cup unsweetened cocoa powder
2 tablespoons water
1 teaspoon vanilla extract

In a mixing bowl, mix margarine and half of confectioners sugar until creamy. Add remaining confectioners sugar and cocoa. Blend until light and fluffy. Add water and vanilla extract. Mix to desired spreading consistency.

Lemon-Poppy Pound Cake

◆M◆E◆P◆S◆N◆

vegetable cooking spray
1 1/4 cups sugar
1/3 cup oil
3 tablespoons oil, 3 tablespoons water,
   2 teaspoons baking powder;
   mixed together
1 1/4 cups water
1/4 cup lemon juice

3 cups flour
1 teaspoon baking powder
1 teaspoon baking soda
1/4 teaspoon salt
2 1/2 tablespoons poppy seeds
1 teaspoon grated lemon peel
2 teaspoons vanilla extract

Preheat oven to 350°. Spray Bundt pan with cooking spray. Combine sugar and oil in a large bowl; beat well with electric mixer. Add water, oil, and baking powder mixture; mix well. Combine water and lemon juice; add to sugar and oil mixture. Set aside.

Combine flour, baking powder, baking soda, salt, and poppy seeds; add to sugar mixture. Mix well. Stir in lemon peel and vanilla extract. Pour batter into Bundt pan. Bake 45 minutes or until a cake tester inserted in center comes out clean. Cool in pan 10 minutes; remove from pan and cool on a wire rack.

Chocolate Banana Marble Ring

◆M◆E◆P◆S◆N◆

vegetable cooking spray
3/4 cup brown sugar, firmly packed
1/2 cup sugar
1/4 cup oil
1 cup mashed ripe banana (about 2 bananas)
3 tablespoons water, 3 tablespoons oil,
   2 teaspoons baking powder; mixed
   together

3 cups flour
1 1/2 teaspoons baking soda
1/2 cup plus 1 tablespoon water
2 teaspoons vanilla extract
1/3 cup Hershey's chocolate syrup
2 tablespoons unsweetened cocoa
   powder

Topping

1/2 cup confectioners sugar, sifted
1 tablespoon water

1 tablespoon unsweetened cocoa
    powder

Preheat oven to 350°. Coat a Bundt pan with cooking spray. In a medium bowl, combine sugars and oil. Add mashed banana; stir together well. Add water, oil, and baking powder mixture. Set aside. In a separate bowl, combine flour and baking soda; blend in with sugar mixture. Add water and vanilla extract and stir.

Combine 1 cup of batter with syrup and 2 tablespoons cocoa; stir well. Divide remaining plain batter into two. Pour half into Bundt pan. Spoon chocolate batter on top. Pour remaining batter over chocolate batter. (You will have three layers: plain on top and bottom, chocolate in the middle.) Bake 45 minutes or until a cake tester inserted in center comes out clean. Cool in Bundt pan 15 minutes. Remove from pan and cool on a wire rack.

To make topping, combine confectioners sugar, water, and cocoa; stir well. Drizzle over cooked cake.

Apricot Cake

Ⓜ Ⓔ Ⓟ Ⓢ Ⓝ

2 1/2 cups flour
1 cup sugar
3 1/2 teaspoons baking powder
1 teaspoon salt
1 tablespoon grated orange peel
3 tablespoons oil

1 1/4 cups water
1 1/2 tablespoons water, 1 1/2 table-
    spoons oil, 1 teaspoon baking
    powder; mixed together
1 1/2 cups canned apricots, drained

Preheat oven to 350°. Grease and flour two loaf pans. Measure all ingredients into large mixer bowl; beat on medium speed. Divide batter into the two pans. Bake 55 minutes or until a cake tester inserted in center comes out clean. Remove cake from pans; cool thoroughly before slicing.

Suggestion: Top with confectioners sugar. If using fresh apricots, adjust sugar to taste.

Strawberry Shortcake

◆M◆E◆P◆S◆N◆

2 cups strawberries	1/2 cup shortening
1/2 cup sugar	3 tablespoons milk-free, soy-free
2 cups flour	margarine
1 teaspoon baking powder	1/4 cup cold water
1/2 teaspoon salt	sugar

Cut strawberries in half, place them in a large bowl, and sprinkle them with sugar. Refrigerate at least one hour. (The sugar will create a syrup.)

Preheat oven to 425°. Grease cookie sheets. Combine flour, baking powder, and salt. Blend in shortening and margarine with a fork or pastry cutter until mixture is crumbly. Drizzle cold water evenly over surface; stir until ingredients are moistened.

On a lightly floured surface, roll dough to 1/8-inch thickness. Sprinkle with sugar. Cut into circles and place on cookie sheets. Bake 10 minutes. Let cool completely before topping with strawberries and syrup.

Double Layer Birthday Cake

◆M◆E◆P◆S◆N◆

3 cups cake flour	3 tablespoons water, 3 tablespoons
1 3/4 cups sugar	oil, 2 teaspoons baking powder;
1 1/4 cups water	mixed together
1/2 cup shortening	1 1/2 teaspoons vanilla extract
2 1/2 teaspoons baking powder	1 teaspoon salt
	Cocoa Frosting (next page)

Preheat oven to 350°. Grease and flour two round cake pans. In a large bowl, combine all ingredients. Using an electric mixer, beat until well mixed, approximately 4 minutes. Pour batter into cake pans. Bake 40 to 45 minutes or until a cake tester inserted in center comes out clean. Cool in pans 10 minutes before removing to wire racks. Frost with Cocoa Frosting when completely cooled.

◆ Milk-Free ◆ Egg-Free ◆ Wheat-Free

Cocoa Frosting

♦ⓂⒺⓌⓅⓈⓃ♦

1/2 cup milk-free, soy-free margarine, softened

2 2/3 cups confectioners sugar

1/2 cup unsweetened cocoa powder

1/4 cup water

1 teaspoon vanilla extract

In large bowl, beat margarine until softened (about 1 minute). Add remaining ingredients. Beat until creamy.

Coconut Pie Crust

♦ⓂⒺⓌⓅⓈⓃ♦

1/4 cup shortening

2 cups coconut flakes

Preheat oven to 300°. In a 9-inch pie pan, combine shortening and coconut. Press evenly to form a crust. Bake 35 minutes or until lightly browned.

—*Paula Bailey*

Pumpkin Pie

♦ⓂⒺⓌⓅⓈⓃ♦

2 cups canned pumpkin

3/4 cup brown sugar, firmly packed

1 1/2 cups water

6 1/2 tablespoons cornstarch

1 teaspoon cinnamon

1/2 teaspoon salt

1/4 teaspoon ground cloves

1/2 teaspoon ginger

pie crust

Preheat oven to 375°. In a medium saucepan, combine all ingredients. Cook over medium heat until mixture begins to thicken, stirring constantly. Pour into pie crust (Coconut Pie Crust works well; see above). Bake 30 minutes or until firm. Remove pie from oven, sprinkle coconut topping on top. Bake 5 more minutes.

Topping (optional)

1/4 cup brown sugar

1/4 cup coconut

Mix brown sugar and coconut. Sprinkle on top of pie.

Cheesecake

Crispy Rice Pie Crust

3 cups crispy rice cereal

1/2 cup plus 1 tablespoon frozen apple juice concentrate, thawed

Place cereal in a 9-inch pie pan. Add apple juice concentrate and mix well. Using the back of a spoon, press evenly into the sides and bottom of the pie pan. Set aside.

Filling

2 pounds firm tofu

3/4 cup honey

1 1/2 teaspoons vanilla extract

1/2 teaspoon cinnamon

In a food processor, combine tofu, honey, vanilla extract, and cinnamon. Process until fluffy. Spoon into pie crust and smooth out the top. Cover loosely with plastic wrap and refrigerate until serving time.

Note: The longer the cheesecake chills, the firmer it will be and the richer it will taste.

⬥ Milk-Free ⬥ Egg-Free ⬥ Wheat-Free

Miscellaneous Dishes

❖❖❖

If sorbets or ices are too frozen, place them in the refrigerator and let them soften to desired consistency before serving.

The sauces and glazes in this section can be used on cookies, cakes, or ice cream.

Raspberry sauce (page 196) may be a good alternative to gravy or cranberry sauce on meat dishes.

Banana Split

◆M◆E◆W◆P◆N◆

1 banana	2 teaspoons sugar
3 strawberries	1/4 teaspoon vanilla extract
blueberries	1/2 cup nondairy creamer
raisins	colored sprinkles or a cherry
1 cup frozen strawberries, thawed	

Split the banana in half lengthwise and place in a shallow bowl. Add the whole strawberries, blueberries, and raisins. Heat the thawed strawberries until lukewarm; add sugar to taste. Put strawberries in a blender and purée. Pour the strawberry mixture over the fruit. Mix sugar, vanilla, and nondairy creamer together in a small bowl. Whip with an electric mixer until frothy (it won't be as thick as whipped cream). Pour it on the fruit and top with colored sprinkles or a cherry.

Note: Hot fudge sauce can be added.

Cantaloupe Sherbet

◆M◆E◆W◆P◆S◆N◆

1 1/2 cups water	2 cups cubed fresh cantaloupe pulp
3/4 cup sugar	(about 2 medium cantaloupes)
	1 tablespoon fresh lemon juice

In a saucepan, combine water and sugar. Boil for 5 minutes. Cool. Purée cantaloupe in an electric blender on high speed. Add the lemon juice and cantaloupe to syrup. Mix thoroughly. Pour into freezer-safe bowl and freeze. Before frozen solid, remove from freezer and beat. Return to freezer. Yields 24 small cups.

Suggestions: If you prefer an ice, pour mixture into small cups and freeze it undisturbed. Use peaches in place of the cantaloupe for peach sherbet.

Playdough

1 cup cornstarch	food coloring
1 pound baking soda	1/8 teaspoon oil
1 cup water	

In a large pot, combine ingredients. Cook over medium heat until mealy. Put on a plate, cover with a damp cloth and allow to cool. Knead, and it's ready for fun. Store in a tightly-covered container.

Do Nothing Putty

1/2 cup white glue	3/4 cup liquid starch

In a medium-size bowl, mix glue and 1/4 cup starch. Stir well. Drain extra starch. Repeat until all starch is used, draining each time. Refrigerate for two hours. Store in plastic container.

Chocolate Ice Cream

3 ripe bananas	3 tablespoons unsweetened cocoa powder
3 tablespoons sugar	1/4 cup powdered soy milk
1/3 cup oil	1/2 cup water

Combine all ingredients with an electric mixer. Mix until well blended. Put mixture into pint-size containers and freeze. Stir after 1 hour; return to freezer.

Note: Add raisins for variety.

Watermelon Ice

◆M◆E◆W◆P◆S◆N◆

2 cups water
1 1/4 cups sugar
4 cups diced and seeded watermelon

6-ounce can concentrated pink
  lemonade

In a saucepan, combine water and sugar. Bring to a boil and cook for 5 minutes. Let it cool. Purée the watermelon in a blender. Mix the watermelon purée with the cooled sugar syrup; add the pink lemonade concentrate and stir well. Pour into serving containers or paper cups and freeze.

Note: This ice is very sweet. It is refreshing and delicious after a spicy dinner like tacos.

Strawberry Slush

◆M◆E◆W◆P◆S◆N◆

2 cups strawberries
1 cup orange juice
1/4 cup frozen lemonade concentrate

1/4 cup water
1 teaspoon sugar
5 ice cubes

In a blender combine strawberries, orange juice, lemonade concentrate, and water. Cover and blend until mixture is smooth. Add sugar. With the blender running, add ice cubes, one at a time. Scrape down sides with a rubber spatula, if necessary. Pour into glasses. Serve immediately.

Suggestion: Substitute peaches, watermelon, or other fruit for strawberries.

Glaze

◆M◆E◆W◆P◆S◆N◆

1/2 cup fruit preserves or jelly

2 tablespoons water

In a small saucepan, heat preserves and water over medium heat until preserves are melted. Remove from heat and force through a sieve to strain out any pieces of fruit or seeds.

Return to heat and cook until mixture reaches a thin coating consistency. Remove from heat and brush on breads or cookies.

Makes 1/2 cup.

Hot Fudge Sauce

6 tablespoons milk-free, soy-free
   margarine
1/2 cup water
4 ounces unsweetened baking chocolate

1 cup sugar
3 tablespoons light corn syrup
1/8 teaspoon salt
2 teaspoons vanilla extract

In a small saucepan, combine margarine and water. Bring to a boil over medium heat, stirring continuously.

Add chocolate; stir occasionally until it melts. Chocolate mixture may be lumpy.

Add sugar, corn syrup, and salt. Boil 5 minutes. Remove from heat and add vanilla. Serve hot.

Makes about 2 cups.

Ice Cream Cones

1 cup sugar
1/3 plus 1/4 cup milk-free, soy-free
   margarine
1/3 cup plus 1/8 cup cold water

1 teaspoon vanilla extract
1/4 teaspoon xanthan gum*
2 1/8 cups tapioca flour

Cream sugar and margarine. Mix in rest of ingredients. Beat at high speed for 10 minutes at whip setting. Pour a cup into a pizzelle waffle iron or krumkake iron. Bake a few minutes and roll into cone shape. Press together.

*Xanthan gum is available from Ener-G Foods and at other health food stores.

—Sherry Dougherty

Watermelon Sorbet

◆M◆ ◆E◆ ◆W◆ ◆P◆ ◆S◆ ◆N◆

6 cups cubed and seeded watermelon   **juice of 1/2 lemon**
1 cup sugar

Blend watermelon with sugar in blender or food processor. Add lemon juice and stir well. Spoon mixture into an ice cube tray and freeze for 1 1/2 hours. Remove and beat until smooth; return to freezer for several hours or overnight. Serve in small bowls and decorate with watermelon balls, if desired. Serves 4 to 6.

Raspberry Sauce

◆M◆ ◆E◆ ◆W◆ ◆P◆ ◆S◆ ◆N◆

2 cups frozen raspberries, thawed   **6 tablespoons confectioners sugar**

Purée raspberries in a blender until very smooth. Whisk in sugar. Taste and add more sugar if needed. Refrigerate until ready to use. Can be kept, covered, up to 2 days in refrigerator. Makes about 1 cup.

Note: This sauce may be a good alternative to gravy or cranberry sauce on meat dishes.

Strawberry Sauce

◆M◆ ◆E◆ ◆W◆ ◆P◆ ◆S◆ ◆N◆

2 cups strawberries, chopped   **water, if needed**
1/2 cup sugar

In a small bowl, combine strawberries and sugar; let stand about 1 hour. In a small saucepan over medium heat, cook berry mixture about 5 minutes, mashing berries as they cook. Add water 1 tablespoon at a time if berries are not very juicy. Serve hot or cold.

Chocolate Dip

◆M◆E◆W◆P◆S◆N◆

2 tablespoons unsweetened cocoa powder
2 teaspoons cornstarch
1/4 cup water
1/3 cup light corn syrup

2 teaspoons sugar
2 tablespoons milk-free, soy-free
  margarine
1 teaspoon vanilla extract

In a small saucepan, combine cocoa and cornstarch. Add water; stir until smooth. Stir in the corn syrup and sugar. Cook over medium heat, stirring continuously, until mixture boils; boil 30 seconds, stirring continuously. Remove from heat; add margarine and stir until melted. Stir in vanilla. Cool mixture to room temperature. Makes 1/2 cup.

Note: Great dip for strawberries or bananas.

Fruit Sorbet

◆M◆E◆W◆P◆S◆N◆

8-ounce can crushed, juice-packed
  pineapple
1 1/2 cups bananas, cut in 1-inch chunks
  and frozen

1 tablespoon honey

Place pineapple and its juice in a stainless steel bowl; freeze for 1 hour. Do not allow to freeze completely. Pour into a blender. Purée 30 seconds. Add frozen banana chunks; purée again. Add honey; purée again. Serve immediately.

Suggestions: Other fruit may be substituted. To save for later use, pour into paper cups and keep in freezer. Let sorbet soften before serving after storing in the freezer.

Coconut Rice Pudding

◆M◆ ◆E◆ ◆W◆ ◆P◆ ◆S◆ ◆N◆

6 cups Coconut Water (recipe below)
1 cup uncooked medium-grain rice
1/2 cup sugar

1/4 teaspoon salt
2 teaspoons vanilla extract

Combine Coconut Water, rice, sugar, and salt in medium saucepan. Cook over medium heat, stirring frequently, until bubbles form around the edge. Reduce heat to low. Cover and simmer about 1 hour, or until rice is tender. Stir occasionally. Stir in vanilla extract. Cover and refrigerate until well chilled, about 3 hours.

Note: Excess Coconut Water can be kept in the refrigerator for later use or can be used as a refreshing coconut drink.

Coconut Water

15-ounce can Coco Lopez Cream of Coconut   5 cans water

Before opening Coco Lopez, shake can well. Pour contents into a large pitcher. Add water. Stir well.

Chocolate Pudding

◆M◆ ◆E◆ ◆W◆ ◆P◆ ◆S◆ ◆N◆

1 cup sugar
1/3 cup unsweetened cocoa powder
5 tablespoons cornstarch
1/4 teaspoon salt

3 cups water
1 tablespoon milk-free, soy-free margarine
1 teaspoon vanilla extract

Combine sugar, cocoa, cornstarch, and salt in a saucepan; mix well. Add water, stirring with a wire whisk until well blended. Bring to a boil over medium heat. Boil 1 minute, stirring constantly. Remove from heat. Stir in margarine and vanilla extract.

Pour into individual cups. Let cool to room temperature. Chill completely in refrigerator before serving.

Notes: For a less sweet taste, reduce sugar by 1/3 cup. This recipe can be used as a pie filling.

Strawberry Ice

◆M◆E◆W◆P◆S◆N◆

1 pint fresh strawberries	1 tablespoon lime juice
1/2 cup confectioners sugar	ice cubes

In a blender, combine strawberries, confectioners sugar, and lime juice. Fill blender with ice cubes, and frappé. Pour into paper cups or serving dishes. Cover and freeze 30 to 45 minutes.

Note: This recipe can be used without freezing. Add more ice to make it frosty.

4th of July Strawberries

◆M◆E◆W◆P◆S◆N◆

2 teaspoons water	blue food coloring
1/2 cup confectioners sugar	fresh strawberries

Put 1 teaspoon water into each of two bowls. Add 1/4 cup confectioners sugar to each bowl. Add food coloring drop by drop to one bowl until desired color is achieved. Mix until smooth. You will have one bowl with white frosting and one with blue frosting. To make red, white, and blue striped strawberries, dip strawberries 2/3 deep into the white frosting. Let harden. Dip strawberries 1/3 into blue frosting.

—*Marguerite Furlong*

Nurse Snookim's Fruit Dip

M E W P S N

2 tablespoons cornstarch
1/4 cup sugar

1 cup pineapple juice
1 1/2 teaspoons lemon juice

In a medium saucepan, mix cornstarch and sugar. Gradually add both juices. Cook over medium heat, stirring constantly, until mixture thickens. Cool completely before using.

Notes: Cornstarch can be replaced by an equal amount of flour. This dip works well as a dip for apples or bananas, and as a topping for muffins.

—Jan Almond

Coffee Can Vanilla Ice Cream

M E W P N

1-pound coffee can and lid, emptied
   and cleaned
3-pound coffee can and lid, emptied
   and cleaned
1 cup milk-free nondairy creamer

1 cup soy milk
1/2 cup sugar
1/2 teaspoon vanilla extract
crushed ice
1 cup rock salt, divided

Put all ingredients except ice and rock salt in the smaller coffee can. Cover with lid. Place smaller can inside the larger can. Pack crushed ice around outside of smaller can. Pour at least 3/4 cup rock salt evenly over ice. Cover the can and tape lid securely.

Roll back and forth on a table for 15 minutes. Open outer can and remove inner can. Remove lid. Scrape the ice cream off the sides of the can and stir the mixture to an even consistency. Replace lid. Drain ice water from larger can.

Insert smaller can and pack with more ice and salt. Roll back and forth for 15 minutes or until can frosts over. Stir and serve. Immediately freeze unused ice cream.

Suggestion: Fruit, crushed cookies, or a bit of coconut milk can be added for variety.

—Sheryl Wallin

Milk-Free Egg-Free Wheat-Free

Peach Sorbet

◆◆◆◆◆◆

1/2 cup orange juice	3 tablespoons sugar
1 large peach, peeled and chopped	2 cups ice

Place all ingredients in a blender. Purée until smooth. Freeze at least 30 minutes, or longer if you desire a hard ice consistency.

Chocolate Fondue

◆◆◆◆◆◆

2 1/2 cups water	1/2 cup unsweetened cocoa powder
3/4 cup confectioners sugar	1 teaspoon vanilla extract
1/4 cup cornstarch	1/4 teaspoon salt

Place all ingredients in a blender and process until smooth. Pour into a saucepan and bring to a boil, stirring constantly. Reduce the heat to low. Stir constantly until very thick and smooth. Transfer to a fondue pot and serve with cut fresh fruit.

Suggestions: This is a great birthday cake alternative. Add more confectioners sugar if sweeter taste is desired.

Melon Sorbet

◆◆◆◆◆◆

1 envelope unflavored gelatin	1/2 cup sugar
1/2 cup water	1 medium-size cantaloupe, cubed

In small saucepan, sprinkle the gelatin over the water and let it soften for 5 minutes. Add the sugar, and stir over low heat until the gelatin and sugar are dissolved. Set aside. Purée cantaloupe in a blender or food processor. Pour the fruit into a stainless steel bowl. Stir in the gelatin mixture. Mix well. Place sorbet in freezer. Allow to freeze until hard around edges (1 to 2 hours). Stir until smooth. Return to freezer until ready to serve.

Note: This may be made in an ice cream maker. Follow manufacturer's instructions.

Raspberry-Orange Ice Drink

M E W P S N

2 cups fresh or frozen raspberries
6-ounce can frozen orange juice
concentrate, thawed and undiluted

2 1/2 cups seltzer water
3 tablespoons confectioners sugar
ice

Combine raspberries, orange juice, and seltzer water in blender; cover and process until smooth. Add sugar and enough ice to fill to top of blender; frappé. More sugar and ice may be added if desired.

Pears in Sweet Sauce

M E W P S N

3 ripe pears
1/2 cup apple cider
1/4 cup pure maple syrup
2 teaspoons lemon juice

1 tablespoon milk-free, soy-free
margarine
1/8 teaspoon ground nutmeg
1/8 teaspoon salt

Peel pears, and cut them lengthwise into eighths. Combine with other ingredients in a medium nonstick skillet over medium-high heat. Simmer, stirring frequently, until pears are tender. Transfer pears to a serving dish. Leave sauce in pan. Cook the sauce over high heat until it reduces to a syrup. Pour sauce over the pears and serve.

Suggestion: This recipe can be served over breakfast foods, as part of dinner, or over desserts.

M Milk-Free E Egg-Free W Wheat-Free

Frozen Fruit Drink

◆M◆E◆W◆P◆S◆N◆

1 cup pineapple juice
1 1/2 cups canned pineapple slices,
    frozen

2 sliced bananas, frozen
1/2 cup frozen blueberries or
    strawberries

Combine all ingredients in blender. Blend until it has a "soft serve" consistency. Serve immediately.

Candy Apples

◆M◆E◆W◆P◆S◆N◆

3 cups confectioners sugar
1/2 cup unsweetened cocoa powder
6 tablespoons water

apples
popsicle sticks

In a large bowl, mix sugar, cocoa powder, and water. Add more water if necessary to make spreadable consistency. Set aside. Insert popsicle sticks into bottoms of apples. Dip apples into chocolate sauce and swirl until well coated. Place on wax paper and refrigerate until ready to eat.

Note: This can easily be turned into a fun party idea. Immediately after dipping apples, have children decorate them with candies such as milk-free, egg-free marshmallows, coconut flakes, or other allowed candy pieces.

Soy Strawberry Smoothie

◆M◆E◆W◆P◆N◆

3/4 pound tofu
16-ounce or 20-ounce bag frozen
    strawberries
1/2 cup sugar

3 tablespoons lemon juice
1/4 cup oil
1 teaspoon vanilla extract

Mix all ingredients together in food processor or blender until smooth. Serve immediately.

—Diane Gianelli

Edible Holiday Ornaments

◆M◆◆E◆◆W◆◆P◆◆S◆◆N◆

1/4 cup milk-free, soy-free margarine, softened
1/3 cup light corn syrup
1 teaspoon vanilla extract

16-ounce package confectioners sugar
red food coloring
confectioners sugar

Combine margarine, corn syrup, and vanilla extract in a mixing bowl; beat until well blended. Add sugar; beat well. Knead by hand until smooth. Divide dough in half; wrap one portion in plastic wrap. Knead food coloring into remaining dough. (Add enough drops to create reddish color.) You should now have one red and one white dough.

Roll each portion to 1/8-inch thickness on a surface sprinkled with confectioners sugar. Cut into desired ornament shapes. Twist some red and some white dough together to make candy canes. Make a hole in top of ornaments. Transfer ornaments to wax paper. Let stand 4 hours. Transfer to wire racks. Let stand at least 24 hours until completely hardened.

Coconut Pudding

◆M◆◆E◆◆W◆◆P◆◆S◆◆N◆

4 cups Coconut Water (see page 198)
3 1/2 cups boiling water
1/2 cup cornstarch

2/3 cup sugar
1/2 teaspoon salt

In a large pot, combine coconut water, boiling water, cornstarch, sugar, and salt. Stir. Cook, stirring constantly, over medium-low heat until sauce thickens. Pour immediately into a pan rinsed in cold water. When completely cool, pour into individual dessert cups. Refrigerate to chill completely before serving.

Basic Marshmallow Frosting

◆M◆ E ◆W◆ P ◆S◆ N

1/3 cup water
1 envelope unflavored gelatin
1/2 cup sugar

2/3 cup sugar cane syrup*
1 teaspoon vanilla extract
food coloring, optional

In a saucepan, mix water, gelatin, and sugar together. Heat until sugar and gelatin are dissolved. Add syrup, vanilla extract, and food coloring if used. Beat with electric mixer on high speed until mixture is thick. Use immediately.

*To make syrup, cook 1 cup pure cane sugar and 1/4 cup water in microwave oven 3 to 5 minutes, or until dissolved.

Note: This will make quite a bit. You can put a little into separate bowls and add food coloring to write "Happy Birthday" or other special messages on the cake. The icing will firm up quickly.

—Tracy Tedes

Strawberry Smoothie

◆M◆ E ◆W◆ P ◆S◆ N

1 cup frozen strawberries
1/2 cup sugar

1 cup orange juice
15 ice cubes

Combine all ingredients and purée in a blender. Serve immediately.

—Marguerite Furlong

Tropical Sorbet

◆M◆ ◆E◆ ◆W◆ ◆P◆ ◆S◆ ◆N◆

1 envelope unflavored gelatin
2/3 cup cold water
1/3 cup sugar
6-ounce can frozen orange juice
   concentrate, undiluted

1 mango, peeled and chunked
1 banana, peeled and chunked
6 ice cubes

In a small saucepan, combine gelatin and water; let stand for 5 minutes. Place saucepan over low heat; stir until the gelatin is completely dissolved. Pour the mixture into a blender. Add remaining ingredients except ice cubes, and blend until light and frothy. Add the ice cubes one at a time, continuing to blend until dissolved. Can be served immediately, or divide the mixture into serving cups and freeze. To serve, thaw slightly.

Strawberry-Coconut Sorbet

◆M◆ ◆E◆ ◆W◆ ◆P◆ ◆S◆ ◆N◆

2 cups strawberries, frozen
3/4 cup coconut juice

1/2 cup confectioners sugar

In blender, chop frozen strawberries until fruit resembles finely shaved ice. With blender running, add coconut juice and sugar. Blend until smooth. Pour into bowl and place in freezer; stir every 30 minutes until ready to serve. For future use, freeze completely and allow to thaw slightly before serving.

Coconut Tapioca Pudding

◆M◆ ◆E◆ ◆W◆ ◆P◆ ◆S◆ ◆N◆

2 1/4 cups coconut milk*
1/4 cup quick-cooking tapioca

1 tablespoon sugar (optional)

Combine the coconut milk, tapioca, and sugar (if used) in a saucepan. Let stand 10 minutes. Bring to a boil over medium heat; stir often. When mixture reaches full boil, remove from heat. Cool 20 minutes. Stir well. Serve warm or refrigerate to cool completely.

*Note: To make coconut milk, mix a 15-ounce can Coco Lopez Cream of Coconut with 2 quarts water. Refrigerate remainder or pour into ice cube trays and freeze to make coconut ices.

Fruit Sailboats

Ⓜ Ⓔ Ⓦ Ⓟ Ⓢ Ⓝ

cantaloupe	cherries
paper sails	grapes
wooden skewers	raisins

Cut cantaloupe into long slices, keeping fruit on the rind. Poke two holes on opposite ends of each paper sail and push a skewer through the holes to form sails. Push a cherry, grape, and raisin onto one end of the skewer. Repeat steps on other end. Stick the skewer into the cantaloupe.

Suggestion: Have children write the names of the ships or use crayons to decorate sails before attaching to skewers. Substitute grapes and cherries with your child's favorite fruit.

Note: Apple slices make good sailboats, too.

Vegetable Dip

Ⓜ Ⓔ Ⓟ Ⓝ

1-pound block tofu	2 tablespoons soy sauce
1/4 teaspoon garlic powder	1/4 cup finely chopped onion

In food processor, mix tofu until smooth. Continue processing and add garlic powder, soy sauce, and onion. Mix well. Pour into serving dish. Chill and serve.

—Melanie Norris

Coconut Sorbet

◆M◆E◆W◆P◆S◆N◆

2 14-ounce cans coconut milk
1 cup coconut flakes

2/3 cup sugar

In heavy saucepan, combine coconut milk, coconut flakes, and sugar. Simmer over low heat until coconut is soft and tender. Let cool. Cover and place in refrigerator until chilled. Pour mixture into large, shallow baking dish. Place dish in freezer. Stir mixture every half-hour until it freezes to desired consistency.

Fruit Dip

◆M◆E◆P◆N◆

1/2 bag egg-free, milk-free marshmallows
1-pound block tofu

1 teaspoon vanilla extract

Melt marshmallows in top of double boiler. Set aside. In food processor, mix tofu until smooth. Combine marshmallows with tofu and add vanilla extract. Stir well. Allow to cool before serving.

Suggestion: Use as dip for grapes, strawberries, sliced apples, and other fruits.

—*Melanie Norris*

Edible Fruit Baskets

◆M◆E◆W◆P◆S◆N◆

2 tablespoons warm water
1/2 cup brown sugar

4 soft corn tortillas
confectioners sugar

Preheat oven to 350°. Combine water and brown sugar to make a syrup. Generously brush syrup on tops and bottoms of tortillas. Fit tortillas into large muffin tins or custard bowls. Bake 10 minutes. Sprinkle with confectioners sugar while still hot; let cool before removing from muffin tins. Fill the baskets with fresh fruit chunks, ices, or sorbets.

Sorbet Fruit Shake

◆M◆E◆W◆P◆S◆N◆

2 to 3 scoops raspberry sorbet
1/2 cup orange juice

1 small banana, cut up

Put all ingredients in blender and process until smooth. Serve immediately.

Suggestion: Use different flavor sorbets, different juices, or different kinds of fresh, sliced fruit, such as peaches, kiwi, and strawberries.

—Judy Scrimenti

Pineapple Slush

◆M◆E◆W◆P◆S◆N◆

2 to 3 cups pineapple juice
1 banana, cut into chunks

3 tablespoons sugar
ice

Place ingredients in blender. Blend or purée until desired consistency. Add more ice for a thicker consistency. Serve immediately.

Rice-Flour Play Dough

◆M◆E◆W◆P◆S◆N◆

1 1/4 cups rice flour
1/2 cup salt
2 teaspoons cream of tartar

1 cup water
1 tablespoon oil
1/4 teaspoon vanilla extract

Mix flour, salt, and cream of tartar in a large pot. Add water and oil. Cook over medium heat until the mixture pulls away from the sides of the pan (about 5 minutes), stirring constantly. Add vanilla extract. Mix thoroughly. Put play dough on a clean surface. When cool enough to handle, knead lightly. Store in airtight container.

Suggestion: To make colored play dough, add food coloring to the water.

More Information

❖❖

To receive more information about food allergies, a sample copy of *Food Allergy News*, or ordering information for wallet-size "How to Read a Label" cards, send a legal-size, self-addressed envelope to

The Food Allergy Network
10400 Eaton Place, Suite 107
Fairfax, VA 22030-5647

1-800-929-4040

For information about Celiac Sprue, contact

Gluten Intolerance Group of North America
P. O. Box 23053
Seattle, WA 98102-0353

1-206-325-6980

Celiac Sprue Association
P. O. Box 31700
Omaha, NE 68131-0700

1-402-558-0600

For a free catalog of special, allergy-free foods and ingredients, write to

Ener-G Foods
P. O. Box 84487
Seattle, WA 98124-5787

1-800-331-5222

Hotlines

National Center for Nutrition & Dietetics
Consumer Nutrition Hotline
1-800-366-1655

The American Academy of Allergy & Immunology
1-800-366-ASMA

The American College of Allergy and Immunology
1-800-842-7777

The American Academy of Pediatrics
1-800-433-9016

Glossary

❖❖

In this section you will find the definitions of terms commonly found on food labels.

Agar-agar A complex carbohydrate extract from several varieties of red seaweed. It has the ability to swell and form a gel. It is used as a gelling agent in foods.

Albumins Natural components of animal products, egg albumin (ovalbumin) is found in the egg white; lactalbumin is found in whey, the liquid part of milk.

The albumins are used as additives in diet supplements, and as stabilizers, thickeners, and texturizers in a variety of foods. They are not safe for persons allergic to egg or milk.

Algae A group of plants that includes seaweed and many single-cell marine and freshwater plants. This group includes some common food additives, including agar-agar alginates and carrageenan.

Alginates Extracts from both red and brown seaweeds, used as emulsifiers to blend ingredients and prevent separation. They can also be used as a gel or thickener.

BHA (butylated hydroxyanisole) and BHT (butylated hydroxytoluene) Synthetic (chemically produced) compounds used as preservatives to prevent or delay the spoilage of fats, oils, and fat-containing foods.

Calcium peroxide Synthetic compound added to flours to ensure uniform quality. It also acts as a bleaching agent to extend the shelf life of flours.

Calcium phosphate, potassium phosphate, sodium phosphate Commercially prepared from phosphoric acid. Used as a flavoring agent and to prevent foods from separating. Used a lot in instant foods. Can also be used to vary acid or alkaline nature of food and as a nutritional supplement.

Calcium stearoyl-2-lactylate and sodium stearoyl-2-lactylate Produced by combining lactic acid and stearic acid, they are used as dough conditioners to produce a more stable, durable dough. Also used as whipping agents for icings and as emulsifiers in coffee creamers and salad dressings.

Caramel Manufactured by the heating of various sugars to produce caramel flavoring or by heating the sugars along with an acid or alkaline salt to produce caramel color.

The sugars that may be used in this process are dextrose, sucrose, molasses, malt syrup, and lactose. Caramel made from lactose would not be safe for milk-allergic persons. Contact the manufacturer to verify the source of the caramel.

Carob A flavoring made from the pods of the carob tree, it has a flavor similar to chocolate but contains no caffeine. Carob is available in powder or chips. Read the label to be sure the carob chips are milk-free.

Carotene, beta-carotene A yellow-orange pigment that is found in fruits and vegetables. Carotene can be converted by the body to vitamin A. In addition to being a nutritional supplement, it is used as a coloring agent.

Carrageenan Also known as Irish moss; it is extracted from a variety of red algae. It, like the alginates, is used as an emulsifier and a stabilizer to keep mixtures from separating and as a gelling and thickening agent.

Casein and caseinates Prepared from a process that uses skim milk to form a casein curd that is washed and dried. Caseinates are then produced by dissolving the casein in an alkaline solution that is sprayed or roller dried.

These substances are used as binders, extenders, clarifying agents, or dietary supplements. They are not safe for milk-allergic persons.

EDTA (ethylenediamine tetraacetic acid), calcium disodium EDTA, and disodium EDTA Chemical compounds that tightly bind to metals, such as copper and iron, that can cause oxidation and rancidity and change the flavor and texture of food. EDTA prevents these reactions and improves stability and shelf life of foods.

Gluten A mixture of proteins present in wheat flour, obtained as an extremely sticky yellowish-gray mass by making a dough and then washing out the starch.

It consists almost entirely of two proteins, gliadin and glutelin, the exact proportions of which depend on the variety of wheat. Gluten contributes to the porous and spongy structure of bread. People with celiac sprue must avoid eating gluten-containing products.

Gum arabic, acacia A gum obtained from a number of species of acacia, a Middle Eastern tree. It is a complex carbohydrate that dissolves in water, thus making it useful as a food additive. It is used as a blender and as a thickener, and improves texture.

Hydrolyzed casein Hydrolyzed casein is made from casein that has been treated with enzymes. It is typically not safe for milk-allergic patients.

Hydrolyzed plant protein (HPP) and hydrolyzed vegetable protein (HVP) Produced either by the hydrolysis of soybean and peanut meals or from protein recovered from the wet milling of grains. Soybeans are the primary source of most HPP and HVP. Contact the manufacturer to determine the source of HPP or HVP.

Lactic acid Produced in commercial foods either by chemical synthesis or from bacterial fermentation of a carbohydrate such as corn sugar.

Lecithin A complex mixture of fatty substances derived primarily from the processing of soybeans, but also from corn and eggs to a lesser extent. The main components of lecithin are choline, phosphoric acid, glycerin, and fatty acids. Manufacturers usually state if egg lecithin is used. When in doubt, call the manufacturer.

Lecithin is used as an emulsifier, a stabilizer, and an antioxidant. Choline is chemically synthesized for use as a food additive. Glycerin is an alcohol that is a component of all fats.

Locust bean gum, also known as carob bean gum or carob seed gum Extracted from the seed of a carob tree. The gum is used as a blender, a stabilizer, and a binder, and to improve the texture of foods.

Malt Produced from germinated barley, malt syrup is a thick concentrate extracted from malt with water. Dried malt extract, a powder, is produced by drying the syrup. It is used to flavor foods and to make breads, beer, and whiskey.

Propionic acid, calcium propionate, and sodium propionate Produced by chemical synthesis for the food industry to inhibit mold growth and to preserve foods.

Protein hydrolysates Mixtures of amino acids (the primary components of proteins) naturally found in foods. They are extracted from foods by various chemical and manufacturing processes.

Sorbitan derivatives, polysorbate 60, 65, 80, sorbitan monostearate Produced by chemically dehydrating sorbitol, a simple sugar-alcohol. They are used as emulsifiers.

Starch, gelatinized starch, modified starch Obtained from a variety of foods: tapioca, potatoes, corn, wheat, and rice. It is produced by steeping and grinding the seed or tuber of the plant to make a slurry to which sulfur dioxide is added to separate the protein from the starch. Starches are used as thickening and gelling agents.

Tapioca A beady starch derived from the root of the tropical cassava plant. Used for puddings and as a thickening agent in cooking.

Tofu White, easily digestible curd made from cooked soybeans. High in protein, it contains no cholesterol. Available in soft (or silken) and firm varieties. It must be avoided by soy-allergic individuals.

Whey The liquid portion of milk that remains after the casein has been removed. It is used in many foods as a source of protein and minerals. Whey should be avoided by milk-allergic persons.

Index

A

Abe Lincoln's Hats, 109
Alissa's Frosted Apple Cookies, 97
Almost French Crepes, 43
Alphabet Cookies, 111–112
American Academy of Allergy & Immunology, 212
American Academy of Pediatrics, 212
American College of Allergy and Immunology, 212
Annie's Granola Bars, 134
apple(s)
    Alissa's Frosted Apple Cookies, 97
    Apple Blondies, 150
    Apple-Butter Spice Cake, 185
    Apple Coffee Cake, 24
    Apple Crisp, 44
    Apple Crunch Muffins, 30
    Apple Fritters, 146
    Apple Muffins with Brown Sugar Sauce, 26–27
    Apple Pie Muffins, 42–43
    Apple-Raisin Bread, 36
    Apple Rings, 24
    Apples and Cornflakes, 30
    Applesauce Bars, 96
    Applesauce Brownies, 182
    Applesauce Muffins, 18–19
    Apple Streusel Muffins, 50–51
    Apple Upside-Down Cake, 170
    Baked Cinnamon Apples, 126–127
    Candy Apples, 203
    Chocolate Applesauce Sheet Cake, 170–171
    Coconut-Apple Pie, 175
    French Apple Tart, 179
    Honey-Apple Pancakes, 14
Apple Blondies, 150
Apple-Butter Spice Cake, 185

Apple Coffee Cake, 24
Apple Crisp, 44
Apple Crunch Muffins, 30
Apple Fritters, 146
Apple Frosting, 97
Apple Muffins with Brown Sugar Sauce, 26–27
Apple Pie Muffins, 42–43
Apple-Raisin Bread, 36
Apple Rings, 24
Apples and Cornflakes, 30
Applesauce Bars, 96
Applesauce Brownies, 182
Applesauce Muffins, 18–19
Apple Streusel Muffins, 50–51
Apple Upside-Down Cake, 170
Apricot Bars, 94
Apricot Cake, 187
apricots
    Apricot Bars, 94
    Apricot Cake, 187
    Moist Apricot Bread, 48
arrowroot, 11
Australian Honey Joys, 106
avocados
    Guacamole, 81

B

Baked Cinnamon Apples, 126–127
Baked Potato Skins, 63
Baking Powder Biscuits, 33
banana(s)
    Banana Bars, 95
    Banana Bread, 20
    Banana Cake, 176
    Banana Frosting, 174
    Banana-Honey Muffins, 37
    Banana Muffins, 18
    Banana Oatmeal Cookies, 112–113
    Banana Rice Bread, 51
    Banana-Rice Pancakes, 16
    Banana Split, 192
    Banana Upside-Down Cake, 172

Chocolate Banana Marble Ring, 186–187
Chocolate-Banana Muffins, 32
Coconut-Banana Coffee Cake, 171
Fried Ripe Bananas, 31
Frozen Fruit Drink, 203
Oat-Banana Bread, 21
Sorbet Fruit Shake, 209
Tropical Sorbet, 206
Banana Bars, 95
Banana Bread, 20
Banana Cake, 176
Banana Frosting, 174
Banana-Honey Muffins, 37
Banana Muffins, 18
Banana Oatmeal Cookies, 112–113
Banana Rice Bread, 51
Banana-Rice Pancakes, 16
Banana Split, 192
Banana Upside-Down Cake, 172
Barley-Carrot Cake, 162
barley flour, 11
Barley-Zucchini Bread, 49
bars
    Annie's Granola Bars, 134
    Apple Blondies, 150
    Applesauce Bars, 96
    Applesauce Brownies, 182
    Apricot Bars, 94
    Banana Bars, 95
    Birthday Brownies, 106
    Butterscotch Bars, 117
    Chewy Bar Cookies, 133
    Christmas Tree, 153–154
    Cookie Bars, 128
    Iced Pumpkin Bars, 131
    Marshmallow Treats, 108
    Pear Blondies, 111
    Puffed Rice Treats, 92
    Raisin Bars, 149
    Raspberry Bars, 95

Rice Krispies Treats, 92
Strawberry Squares, 94
Basic Marshmallow Frosting, 205
beef
  Stove-Top Beef Noodle Casserole, 78
beverages
  Frozen Fruit Drink, 203
  Raspberry-Orange Ice Drink, 202
  Soy Strawberry Smoothie, 203
  Strawberry Smoothie, 205
Birthday Brownies, 106
biscuits
  Baking Powder Biscuits, 33
  Cinnamon Biscuits, 27
  Sweet Potato Biscuits, 72
Black Forest Cake, 157
blueberries
  Blueberry Corn Muffins, 35
  Blueberry Muffins, 19
  Frozen Fruit Drink, 203
Blueberry Corn Muffins, 35
Blueberry Muffins, 19
Bread Bowls, 45
breads. See also corn bread/cornmeal
  Apple-Raisin Bread, 36
  Baking Powder Biscuits, 33
  Banana Bread, 20
  Banana Rice Bread, 51
  Barley-Zucchini Bread, 49
  Bread Bowls, 45
  Butternut Squash Loaf, 72–73
  Cinnamon Biscuits, 27
  Cranberry Bread, 46–47
  Crunchy Breakfast Bread, 32–33
  David's Corn Bread, 73
  David's Favorite French Bread, 36
  English Muffin Bread, 22
  Honey Breakfast Bread, 31
  Moist Apricot Bread, 48
  Oat-Banana Bread, 21
  Oatmeal-Raisin Loaf, 37–38
  Peach Breakfast Bread, 20
  Pizza Bread, 76
  Pumpkin Bread, 48
  Raisin Bread, 38
  Rye Bread Sticks, 55
  Tea Loaf, 49
  Zucchini Bread, 22
breakfast food. See coffee cakes; french toast; muffins; pancakes
Breakfast Puffs, 45
Brett's Gingerbread Men, 91
broccoli
  Broccoli Salad, 80
  Caribbean Fritters, 67
Broccoli Salad, 80
Brown-edged Wafers, 116–117
brownies
  Applesauce Brownies, 182
  Birthday Brownies, 106

Brown Sugar Sauce, 27
Butternut Squash Loaf, 72–73
Butterscotch Bars, 117

C
cakes/cup cakes. See also coffee cakes
  Apple-Butter Spice Cake, 185
  Apple Upside-Down Cake, 170
  Apricot Cake, 187
  Banana Cake, 176
  Banana Upside-Down Cake, 172
  Barley-Carrot Cake, 162
  Black Forest Cake, 157
  Cheesecake, 190
  Chocolate Applesauce Sheet Cake, 170–171
  Chocolate Banana Marble Ring, 186–187
  Chocolate Date Cake, 184
  Chocolate Fudge Cake, 176–177
  Chocolate Pound Cake, 183
  Chocolate Wacky Cupcakes, 183
  Double Layer Birthday Cake, 188
  Fudge Upside-Down Cake, 163
  Funnel Cakes, 135
  Gingerbread Cake, 184
  Halloween Cupcakes, 161
  Heavenly Chocolate Cupcakes, 180
  Ho Ho Sheet Cake, 158
  Lemon-Poppy Pound Cake, 186
  Moist Spice Cake, 169
  Morning Glory Cake, 167
  Orange Cupcakes, 163
  Pear Cake, 159
  Snacking Cake, 177
  Spring Basket Cupcakes, 160
  Strawberry Cake, 156
  Strawberry Shortcake, 188
  Swirl Cake, 179–180
  Three-Layer Chocolate Cake, 182
  Triple-Layer Chocolate Coconut Cake, 168
  Valentine Cupcakes, 175
  Wacky Chocolate Cake, 160
  White Birthday Cake, 162
  White Cake, 178
candy
  Candy Apples, 203
  Chocolate Fudge, 147
  Fudge Balls, 91
Candy Apples, 203
Candy Cane Cookies, 104–105
Cantaloupe Sherbet, 192
Caramel Cookies, 147
Caramel Crunch, 150
Caramel Glaze, 25
Caramel Popcorn, 93
Caribbean Fritters, 67

Carol's Cheese-Free Pizza Topping, 69
Carol's Spicy Barbecue Sauce, 70
Carrot Breakfast Muffins, 39
Carrot Cake, 156–157
carrots
  Barley-Carrot Cake, 162
  Carrot Breakfast Muffins, 39
  Carrot Cake, 156–157
  Snacking Cake, 177
casseroles
  Greg's Nacho Casserole, 62
  Pineapple Sweet Potato Casserole, 58
  Stove-Top Beef Noodle Casserole, 78
Celiac Sprue Association, 211
cereals
  Apples and Cornflakes, 30
  Granola, 96
Cheesecake, 190
Cherry-in-the-Middle Cookies, 101–102
Chewy Bar Cookies, 133
chicken
  Chicken and Rice, 61
  Fajitas, 81
  Kathy's Barbecued Wings, 77
Chicken and Rice, 61
Chocolate Applesauce Sheet Cake, 170–171
Chocolate Banana Marble Ring, 186–187
Chocolate-Banana Muffins, 32
Chocolate-Cherry Butter Ball Cookies, 142
Chocolate Cookies, 137–138
Chocolate Crisps, 134–135
Chocolate Date Cake, 184
Chocolate Dip, 197
Chocolate Drop Cookies, 104
Chocolate Fondue, 201
Chocolate Frosting, 157
Chocolate Fudge, 147
Chocolate Fudge Cake, 176–177
Chocolate Ice Cream, 193
Chocolate Pancakes, 29
Chocolate Pound Cake, 183
Chocolate Pretzels, 107
Chocolate Pudding, 198
Chocolate Snap Cookies, 110
Chocolate Snickerdoodle Cookies, 141
Chocolate Valentine's Day Cookies, 99
Chocolate Wacky Cupcakes, 183
Christmas Tree, 153–154
Cinnamon Biscuits, 27
Cinnamon Bubbles, 143
Cinnamon-Chocolate Frosting, 164
Cinnamon Cookies, 98–99
Cinnamon Crunch Cookies, 86
Cinnamon Raisin Coffee Cake, 23
Cinnamon Swirl Coffee Cake, 42
Cinnamon Syrup, 130

Index

Cinnamon Topping, 25
Cinnamuffins, 18
Cocoa Frosting, 189
Cocoa-Gingerbread Cookies, 124
Coconut-Apple Pie, 175
Coconut-Banana Coffee Cake, 171
Coconut Cookies, 98
Coconut Pie Crust, 189
Coconut Pudding, 204
Coconut Rice Pudding, 198
Coconut Scones, 127–128
Coconut Sorbet, 208
Coconut Tapioca Pudding, 206–207
coffee cakes. *See also* cakes/cup cakes
  Apple Coffee Cake, 24
  Cinnamon Raisin Coffee Cake, 23
  Cinnamon Swirl Coffee Cake, 42
  Coconut-Banana Coffee Cake, 171
  George Washington's Cherry Coffee Cake, 54
  Pear Coffee Cake, 44
Coffee Can Vanilla Ice Cream, 200
Cold Pasta Salad, 80
Cold Sesame Noodles, 71
Colorful Coconut Icing, 165
Colorful Sprinkle Cookies, 115
Cookie Bars, 128
cookies
  Abe Lincoln's Hats, 109
  Alissa's Frosted Apple Cookies, 97
  Alphabet Cookies, 111–112
  Australian Honey Joys, 106
  Banana Oatmeal Cookies, 112–113
  Brett's Gingerbread Men, 91
  Brown-edged Wafers, 116–117
  Candy Cane Cookies, 104–105
  Caramel Cookies, 147
  Cherry-in-the-Middle Cookies, 101–102
  Chocolate-Cherry Butter Ball Cookies, 142
  Chocolate Cookies, 137–138
  Chocolate Crisps, 134–135
  Chocolate Drop Cookies, 104
  Chocolate Snap Cookies, 110
  Chocolate Snickerdoodle Cookies, 141
  Chocolate Valentine's Day Cookies, 99
  Cinnamon Bubbles, 143
  Cinnamon Cookies, 98–99
  Cinnamon Crunch Cookies, 86
  Cocoa-Gingerbread Cookies, 124
  Coconut Cookies, 98
  Colorful Sprinkle Cookies, 115
  Creamy Sandwich Cookies, 122
  Crescent Cookies, 144
  Crispy Oatmeal Cookies, 118
  Crunchy Shortbread Cookies, 115
  Dusted Chocolate Cookies, 114–115
  Easy Oatmeal Cookies, 86–87
  4th of July Cookies, 101
  Friendship Cookies, 140
  Fruity Cookies, 89
  Fudgie Chocolate Sugar Cookies, 118
  George Washington's Cherry Cookies, 125
  Gingerbread Cookies, 114
  Gingersnap Cookies, 87–88
  Gingersnap Oat Cookies, 128–129
  Gingersnaps, 130
  Halloween Cookie Pops, 152
  Halloween Cookies, 119
  Hermits, 133
  Holiday Cookies, 107
  Holiday Cut-Out Cookies, 90
  Holiday Slices, 123
  Laura's Christmas Cookies, 103
  Lunchbox Cookies, 126
  Maple Cookies, 148
  Maple Crunchies, 132
  Marquerite's St. Patrick's Day Shamrocks, 100
  Molasses Cookies, 120
  Mourning Dove Cookies, 132
  Nana Cookies, 142
  Oatmeal Cookies, 87
  Old-Fashioned Cookies, 89
  Old-Fashioned Holiday Cookies, 120
  Old-Fashioned Oatmeal Cookies, 135
  Pastel Melt Away Cookies, 88
  Poppy Seed Cookies, 151
  Pumpkin Cookies, 112
  Robin's Nest Cookies, 108
  Russian Tea Cookies, 90
  Sandwich Cookies, 113
  Sesame Sweethearts, 144
  Shortbread Crescents, 121
  Snowballs, 102
  Snow White Cookies, 145
  Stained Glass Cookies, 103–104
  Stick Cookies, 141
  Sugar & Spice Cookies, 139
  Sweet Heart Cookies, 138
  Sweetheart Cookies, 109–110
  Tree Lights, 153
  Tropical Cookies, 136–137
  Vanilla-Coconut Cookies, 139
  Vanilla Cookies, 127, 148
  Vanilla Rainbow Cookies, 136
  Vanilla Spritz Cookies, 143
  Wafers, 116
  Yummy Crinkles Cookies, 137
  Zebra Cookies, 124–125
cooking tips, 2–3
corn bread/cornmeal
  Caribbean Fritters, 67
  Corn Cakes, 53
  Corn Muffins, 21
  David's Corn Bread, 73
  Hush Puppies, 67
  Northern-Style Corn Bread, 75
Corn Cakes, 53
Cornflake Crumb Crust, 166
corn flour, 11
Corn Muffins, 21
cornstarch, 11
Cranberry Bread, 46–47
Cranberry Muffins, 50
Cream of Mushroom Soup, 60
Cream Sauce, 59
Creamy Cocoa Frosting, 185
Creamy Frosting, 169
Creamy Sandwich Cookies, 122
Creamy Vanilla Frosting, 181
crepes
  Almost French Crepes, 43
Crescent Cookies, 144
Crispy Oatmeal Cookies, 118
Crunchy Breakfast Bread, 32–33
Crunchy Shortbread Cookies, 115

D

David's Corn Bread, 73
David's Favorite French Bread, 36
Decadent Chocolate Frosting, 181
Deep-Dish Pizza Dough, 68
dips
  Chocolate Dip, 197
  Chocolate Fondue, 201
  Fruit Dip, 208
  Nurse Snookim's Fruit Dip, 200
  Vegetable Dip, 207
Do Nothing Putty, 193
Double Layer Birthday Cake, 188
Doughnut Holes, 105
doughnuts
  Doughnut Holes, 105
  Powdered Sugar Doughnut, 173
  Pumpkin Doughnuts, 47
Dusted Chocolate Cookies, 114–115

E

Easy Oatmeal Cookies, 86–87
Easy Vegetable Soup, 75
Edible Fruit Baskets, 208
Edible Holiday Ornaments, 204
egg-free diet
  reading labels for, 4–5
egg substitutes, 9
Ener-G Foods, 211
English Muffin Bread, 22

F

Fajitas, 81
fish
    Tuna Rolls, 58
    Tuna Soup, 65
flour
    gliadin-free, 10–11
    gluten-free, 10–11
    types of, 11–12
    wheat-free all purpose flour
        mixture, 12
flour substitutes, 10–11
Food Allergy Network, 211
4th of July Cookies, 101
4th of July Strawberries, 199
French Apple Tart, 179
french toast
    Orange-Flavored French
        Toast, 17
Fried Potatoes, 62
Fried Ripe Bananas, 31
Friendship Cookies, 140
frostings. See also glazes; top-
        pings
    Apple Frosting, 97
    Banana Frosting, 174
    Basic Marshmallow Frosting,
        205
    Chocolate Frosting, 157
    Cinnamon-Chocolate
        Frosting, 164
    Cocoa Frosting, 189
    Colorful Coconut Icing, 165
    for cookies, 154
    Creamy Cocoa Frosting, 185
    Creamy Frosting, 169
    Creamy Vanilla Frosting, 181
    Decadent Chocolate
        Frosting, 181
    Fudge Frosting, 174
    Green Icing, 100
    for Iced Pumpkin Bars, 131
    Lemon Frosting, 164, 178
    Minty Frosting, 180
    Orange Frosting, 161
    Orange Icing, 119
    Pumpkin Frosting, 174
    for Sandwich Cookies, 113
    Smooth Chocolate Frosting,
        181
    for Snow White Frosting, 145
    Valentine Frosting, 175–176
    Vanilla Coconut Frosting, 168
    Vanilla Frosting, 164
    Vanilla Icing, 23, 26
Frozen Fruit Drink, 203
frozen treats
    Banana Split, 192
    Cantaloupe Sherbet, 192
    Chocolate Ice Cream, 193
    Coconut Sorbet, 208
    Coffee Can Vanilla Ice Cream,
        200
    Frozen Fruit Drink, 203
    Fruit Sorbet, 197
    Ice Cream Cones, 195
    Melon Sorbet, 201
    Peach Sorbet, 201
    Pineapple Slush, 209

Sorbet Fruit Shake, 209
Soy Strawberry Smoothie,
    203
Strawberry-Coconut Sorbet,
    206
Strawberry Ice, 199
Strawberry Slush, 194
Strawberry Smoothie, 205
Tropical Sorbet, 206
Watermelon Ice, 194
Watermelon Sorbet, 196
Fruit and Popcorn Snack, 93–94
Fruit Crisp, 172
Fruit Dip, 208
Fruit Sailboats, 207
Fruit Sorbet, 197
Fruity Cookies, 89
fudge
    Chocolate Fudge, 147
    Fudge Balls, 91
Fudge Frosting, 174
Fudge Upside-Down Cake, 163
Fudgie Chocolate Sugar
    Cookies, 118
Funnel Cakes, 135

G

George Washington's Cherry
    Coffee Cake, 54
George Washington's Cherry
    Cookies, 125
Gingerbread Cake, 184
Gingerbread Cookies, 114
Gingersnap Cookies, 87–88
Gingersnap Oat Cookies,
    128–129
Gingersnaps, 130
Glaze, 194–195
Glazed Peach Pie, 165
Glazed Strawberry Pie, 167
glazes. See also frostings; top-
        pings
    Caramel Glaze, 25
    Glaze, 194–195
    Honey Glaze, 25
    Lemon Glaze, 50
    Orange Glaze, 25
    for Pastel Melt Away Cookies,
        88
Gluten Intolerance Group of
    North America, 211
Gnocchi di Patate, 69
Golden Brown Muffins, 28
Granola, 96
Green Icing, 100
Greg's Nacho Casserole, 62
Guacamole, 81

H

Halloween Cookie Pops, 152
Halloween Cookies, 119
Halloween Cupcakes, 161
Healthy Breakfast Muffins, 40
Heavenly Chocolate Cupcakes,
    180
Hermits, 133
Hidden Surprise Muffins, 17
Ho Ho Sheet Cake, 158
Holiday Cookies, 107
Holiday Cut-Out Cookies, 90

Holiday Slices, 123
Home-Style Pancakes, 15
Honey-Apple Pancakes, 14
Honey Breakfast Bread, 31
Honey Glaze, 25
Hot Fudge Sauce, 195
Hush Puppies, 67

I

ice cream. See frozen treats
Ice Cream Cones, 195
Iced Pumpkin Bars, 131
icing. See frostings

J

James's Favorite Pizza Crust,
    78–79
Jelly-Filled Muffins, 53

K

Kathy's Barbecued Wings, 77
kosher symbols, 2

L

labels
    for egg-free diet, 4–5
    for milk-free diet, 3–4
    for peanut-free diet, 6–7
    for soy-free diet, 7–8
    for tree nut allergy, 8–9
    for wheat-free diet, 5–6
Lasagna, 60
Laura's Christmas Cookies, 103
Lemon Frosting, 164, 178
Lemon Glaze, 50
Lemon-Poppy Pound Cake, 186
Lunchbox Cookies, 126

M

Maple-Cider Sauce, 47
Maple Cookies, 148
Maple Crunchies, 132
Marguerite's St. Patrick's Day
    Shamrocks, 100
Marshmallow Treats, 108
Melon Sorbet, 201
Middle Eastern Pizza Topping,
    79
milk-free diet
    kosher symbols and, 2
    reading labels for, 3–4
milk substitutes, 10
Minty Frosting, 180
Moist Apricot Bread, 48
Moist Halloween Muffins, 41
Moist Rice Stuffing, 82
Moist Spice Cake, 169
Molasses Cookies, 120
Morning Glory Cake, 167
Mourning Dove Cookies, 132
muffins
    Apple Crunch Muffins, 30
    Apple Muffins with Brown
        Sugar Sauce, 26–27
    Apple Pie Muffins, 42–43
    Applesauce Muffins, 18–19
    Apple Streusel Muffins,
        50–51
    Banana-Honey Muffins, 37
    Banana Muffins, 18
    Blueberry Corn Muffins, 35

Index

Blueberry Muffins, 19
Breakfast Puffs, 45
Carrot Breakfast Muffins, 39
Chocolate-Banana Muffins, 32
Cinnamuffins, 18
Corn Muffins, 21
Cranberry Muffins, 50
Golden Brown Muffins, 28
Healthy Breakfast Muffins, 40
Hidden Surprise Muffins, 17
Jelly-Filled Muffins, 53
Moist Halloween Muffins, 41
Peachy Muffins, 52
Pear Muffins, 34
Poppyseed Muffins, 66
Raspberry Cinnamon Muffins, 39
Rye Muffins, 33
Sticky Muffins, 40
Sweet Oatmeal Muffins, 28
Sweet Potato Muffins, 66
Zesty Zucchini Muffins, 35

N

Nana Cookies, 142
National Center for Nutrition & Dietetics, 212
Northern-Style Corn Bread, 75
Nurse Snookim's Fruit Dip, 200

O

Oat-Banana Bread, 21
Oatmeal Cookies, 87
Oatmeal-Raisin Loaf, 37–38
Oat Pancakes, 14
Old-Fashioned Cookies, 89
Old-Fashioned Holiday Cookies, 120
Old-Fashioned Oatmeal Cookies, 135
Orange Cupcakes, 163
Orange-Flavored French Toast, 17
Orange Frosting, 161
Orange Glaze, 25
Orange Icing, 119
ornaments
Edible Holiday Ornaments, 204

P

pancakes
Banana-Rice Pancakes, 16
Chocolate Pancakes, 29
Home-Style Pancakes, 15
Honey-Apple Pancakes, 14
Oat Pancakes, 14
Potato Pancakes, 16
Rice Flour Griddle Cakes, 15
Parsley-Potato Stuffing, 64
pasta
Cold Pasta Salad, 80
Cold Sesame Noodles, 71
Lasagna, 60
Pastel Melt Away Cookies, 88
peach(s)
Fruit Crisp, 172
Glazed Peach Pie, 165
Peach Breakfast Bread, 20

Peach Sorbet, 201
Peachy Muffins, 52
Peach Breakfast Bread, 20
Peach Sorbet, 201
Peachy Muffins, 52
peanut-free diet
reading labels for, 6–7
pear(s)
Pear Blondies, 111
Pear Cake, 159
Pear Coffee Cake, 44
Pear Muffins, 34
Pear Pie, 173
Pears in Sweet Sauce, 202
Pear Blondies, 111
Pear Cake, 159
Pear Coffee Cake, 44
Pear Muffins, 34
Pear Pie, 173
Pears in Sweet Sauce, 202
pies
Coconut-Apple Pie, 175
Coconut Pie Crust, 189
Cornflake Crumb Crust, 166
French Apple Tart, 179
Glazed Peach Pie, 165
Glazed Strawberry Pie, 167
Pear Pie, 173
Pumpkin Cake, 189
Rice Pie Crust, 165
Rye Pie Crust, 166
pineapple
Frozen Fruit Drink, 203
Moist Halloween Muffins, 41
Pineapple Slush, 209
Pineapple Sweet Potato Casserole, 58
Snacking Cake, 177
Pineapple Slush, 209
Pineapple Sweet Potato Casserole, 58
pizza
Carol's Cheese-Free Pizza Topping, 69
Deep-Dish Pizza Dough, 68
James's Favorite Pizza Crust, 78–79
Middle Eastern Pizza Topping, 79
Pizza Bread, 76
Pizza Sauce, 76
Wheat-Free Pizza Dough, 68
Pizza Bread, 76
Pizza Sauce, 76
Pizza Topping, 76–77
Playdough, 193
play dough
Do Nothing Putty, 193
Playdough, 193
Rice-Flour Play Dough, 209
popcorn
Caramel Popcorn, 93
Fruit and Popcorn Snack, 93–94
Poppy Seed Cookies, 151
Poppyseed Muffins, 66
Poppy Topping for Baked Breads, 26
Potato Chips, 82

potatoes
Baked Potato Skins, 63
Fried Potatoes, 62
Gnocchi di Patate, 69
Potato Chips, 82
Potato Fans, 81
Potato Pancakes, 16
Potato Puffs, 70
Potato Stuffing, 74
Skillet Potatoes, 78
Potato Fans, 81
potato flour, 12
Potato Pancakes, 16
Potato Puffs, 70
potato starch flour, 12
Potato Stuffing, 74
Powdered Sugar Doughnut, 173
Pretzels, 93
pretzels
Chocolate Pretzels, 107
Sweet Pretzels, 117
pudding
Chocolate Pudding, 198
Coconut Pudding, 204
Coconut Rice Pudding, 198
Coconut Tapioca Pudding, 206–207
Puffed Rice Treats, 92
pumpkin
Iced Pumpkin Bars, 131
Moist Halloween Muffins, 41
Pumpkin Bread, 48
Pumpkin Cake, 189
Pumpkin Cookies, 112
Pumpkin Doughnuts, 47
Pumpkin Bread, 48
Pumpkin Cake, 189
Pumpkin Cookies, 112
Pumpkin Doughnuts, 47
Pumpkin Frosting, 174

R

Raisin Bars, 149
Raisin Bread, 38
raspberries
Raspberry Bars, 95
Raspberry Cinnamon Muffins, 39
Raspberry-Orange Ice Drink, 202
Raspberry Sauce, 196
Raspberry Bars, 95
Raspberry Cinnamon Muffins, 39
Raspberry-Orange Ice Drink, 202
Raspberry Sauce, 196
rice
Chicken and Rice, 61
Moist Rice Stuffing, 82
rice flour, 12
Rice Flour Griddle Cakes, 15
Rice-Flour Play Dough, 209
Rice Krispies Treats, 92
Rice Pie Crust, 165
Robin's Nest Cookies, 108
Russian Tea Cookies, 90
Rye Bread Sticks, 55
rye flour, 12

Rye Muffins, 33
Rye Pie Crust, 166

S
salads
Broccoli Salad, 80
Cold Pasta Salad, 80
Greg's Nacho Casserole, 62
Sandwich Cookies, 113
sauces
Brown Sugar Sauce, 27
Carol's Spicy Barbecue
Sauce, 70
Chocolate Dip, 197
Cinnamon Syrup, 130
Cream Sauce, 59
Guacamole, 81
Hot Fudge Sauce, 195
Maple-Cider Sauce, 47
Nurse Snookim's Fruit Dip,
200
Pizza Sauce, 76
Raspberry Sauce, 196
Spaghetti Sauce, 63
Strawberry Sauce, 29, 196
scones
Coconut Scones, 127–128
Sticky Scones, 129
Streusel-Oat Scones, 46
Sesame-Sunflower Tahini, 71
Sesame Sweethearts, 144
Sesame Topping for Baked
Breads, 26
Shortbread Crescents, 121
Skillet Potatoes, 78
Smooth Chocolate Frosting,
181
Snacking Cake, 177
snack mix
Caramel Crunch, 150
Tacky Snax, 129
Snowballs, 102
Snow White Cookies, 145
Snow White Frosting, 145
Sorbet Fruit Shake, 209
soups
Cream of Mushroom Soup,
60
Easy Vegetable Soup, 75
Tuna Soup, 65
Turkey Soup, 59
Vegetable Soup, 64
soy flour, 12
soy-free diet
reading labels for, 7–8
Soy Strawberry Smoothie, 203
Spaghetti Sauce, 63
spices
organizing, 2
Spring Basket Cupcakes, 160
squash
Butternut Squash Loaf,
72–73
Stained Glass Cookies, 103–104
Stick Cookies, 141
Sticky Muffins, 40
Sticky Scones, 129
Stove-Top Beef Noodle
Casserole, 78

strawberries
4th of July Strawberries, 199
Frozen Fruit Drink, 203
Glazed Strawberry Pie, 167
Soy Strawberry Smoothie,
203
Strawberry Cake, 156
Strawberry-Coconut Sorbet,
206
Strawberry Ice, 199
Strawberry Sauce, 29, 196
Strawberry Shortcake, 188
Strawberry Slush, 194
Strawberry Smoothie, 205
Strawberry Squares, 94
Strawberry Cake, 156
Strawberry-Coconut Sorbet,
206
Strawberry Ice, 199
Strawberry Sauce, 29, 196
Strawberry Shortcake, 188
Strawberry Slush, 194
Strawberry Smoothie, 205
Strawberry Squares, 94
Streusel-Oat Scones, 46
Streusel Topping, 37, 51
stuffing
Moist Rice Stuffing, 82
Parsley-Potato Stuffing, 64
Potato Stuffing, 74
substitutes
egg, 9
flour, 10–11
general, 9
milk, 10
Sugar & Spice Cookies, 139
Sweet Heart Cookies, 138
Sweetheart Cookies, 109–110
Sweet Oatmeal Muffins, 28
Sweet Potato Biscuits, 72
sweet potatoes
Pineapple Sweet Potato
Casserole, 58
Sweet Potato Biscuits, 72
Sweet Potato Muffins, 66
Sweet Potato Muffins, 66
Sweet Pretzels, 117
Swirl Cake, 179–180
syrup
Cinnamon Syrup, 130

T
Tacky Snax, 129
tahini
Sesame-Sunflower Tahini, 71
tapioca flour, 12
Tea Loaf, 49
Three-Layer Chocolate Cake,
182
toppings. See also frostings;
glazes
Cinnamon Topping, 25
for Fudge Upside-Down Cake,
163
Middle Eastern Pizza
Topping, 79
for Peachy Muffins, 52
Pizza Topping, 76–77
Poppy or Sesame Topping for

Baked Breads, 26
for Raisin Bars, 149
Streusel Topping, 37, 51
Wheat-Free Coating, 83
Tree Lights, 153
tree nut allergy
reading labels for, 8–9
Triple-Layer Chocolate Coconut
Cake, 168
Tropical Cookies, 136–137
Tropical Sorbet, 206
Tuna Rolls, 58
Tuna Soup, 65
Turkey Seasoning, 74
Turkey Soup, 59
Turkey Tots, 65

V
Valentine Cupcakes, 175
Valentine Frosting, 175–176
Vanilla-Coconut Cookies, 139
Vanilla Coconut Frosting, 168
Vanilla Cookies, 127, 148
Vanilla Frosting, 164
Vanilla Icing, 23, 26
Vanilla Rainbow Cookies, 136
Vanilla Spritz Cookies, 143
Vegetable Dip, 207
Vegetable Soup, 64

W
Wacky Chocolate Cake, 160
Wafers, 116
Watermelon Ice, 194
Watermelon Sorbet, 196
wheat-free all-purpose flour
mixture, 12
Wheat-Free Coating, 83
wheat-free diet
reading labels for, 5–6
wheat-free all purpose flour
mixture, 12
Wheat-Free Pizza Dough, 68
White Birthday Cake, 162
White Cake, 178

X
xanthan gum, 11

Y
Yummy Crinkles Cookies, 137

Z
Zebra Cookies, 124–125
Zesty Zucchini Muffins, 35
zucchini
Barley-Zucchini Bread, 49
Zesty Zucchini Muffins, 35
Zucchini Bread, 22
Zucchini Bread, 22